CHESSMEN

A.E.J. MACKETT–BEESON

 OCTOPUS BOOKS

Acknowledgements

Contents

The author desires to express his thanks to the following collectors for the use of some of the chesspieces shown in this work, and especially to David Hafler Esq., USA and John Harbison Esq., USA for their untiring efforts on his behalf. The illustrations are reproduced by kind permission of Samuel Bronstein Esq., USA; Sol Solus-Chaken Esq., USA; David Hafler Esq., USA; John Jaques Esq., London; Dr Michael Langford, London; Mrs Edith Liddell-Twiss, USA (from the Liddell Collection); Russell M. Posner Esq., USA; Schuyler Van Rensselaer Camman Esq., USA; Dr J.G. Wurfbain.

Also to the authorities, directors and curators of the following museums; The British Museum, London; The Salisbury and South Wiltshire Museum, Salisbury; The Nationalmuseet, Copenhagen K., Denmark; Statens Historiska Museum, Stockholm, Sweden; The Yorkshire Museum, Yorkshire; to The Ministry of Public Building and Works, London; and to Messrs Christies, London; Messrs Sothebys, London; Messrs Spink & Sons, London; Messrs Wartski (Kenneth Snowman Esq.), London; and to Messrs Faber & Faber, London, for their kind cooperation.

Considerable credit is due to Larry Fritz, of Fritz Creative Services, Merion Station, Pennsylvania, USA for his kindness and skill when photographing many of the chesspieces shown.

This edition first published 1973 by
OCTOPUS BOOKS LIMITED
59 Grosvenor Street, London W.1

ISBN 0 7064 0050 X

© 1967 by George Weidenfeld and Nicolson Ltd

Produced by Mandarin Publishers Limited
77a Marble Road, North Point, Hong Kong
Printed in Hong Kong

Preceding page
Pieces from a Delhi set made in Indian ivory in 1800; the pieces of the black side are stained.

A BRIEF HISTORY OF CHESS

1 Engraving after a medieval painting showing a chess game in progress.

THE GAME of chess, its origin, evolution and progression through countries of the Old World has, for centuries, fascinated and stirred the imagination of chess players and historians. Since Caxton printed his immortal *The Game and Playe Of Chesse*, translated from the French, in 1474, innumerable books have been written on the subject and it is small wonder that chess has been designated 'The Royal Game'.

To befit such a game, craftsmen of many countries designed and produced exquisite chesspieces from an enormous variety of substances including wood, bone, ivory, amber, hardstones, gold, silver, brass, copper, iron and pewter. In addition, several of the most celebrated pottery and porcelain factories have produced delightful sets. Before we can fully appreciate chess as a game, and the delight of beautiful chesspieces, we must know a little of the history of the game and the development of the pieces.

In its earliest form, chess was a board game played by four persons, each of whom controlled eight chesspieces; a king, a rook, a knight and a bishop, together with four pawns. The chessboard was subdivided into sixty-four squares. At the beginning of a game, the four sets of chesspieces occupied positions on the board as shown in figure 3.

This was chess in its infancy, and instead of the conventional pieces as known and used today, the rook was an elephant, the knight a horse, the bishop a ship (later to become a chariot) and the pawns were foot-soldiers. A bishop occupied the left-hand square of the rear rank, next to him stood a knight, then a rook and then a king. The pawns occupied four squares in the second rank, one in front of each major piece. Each player used pieces of his own colour: one yellow, one green, one red, and the other black.

At the beginning of a game, the two opposite players were allied against the other pair and the moves were decided by the throw of a four-sided die. Each face of the die was marked with a different number: one with a two, one with a three, one with a four and one with a five. The two and five were opposites, as were the three and four. When the die was thrown, if a five

3

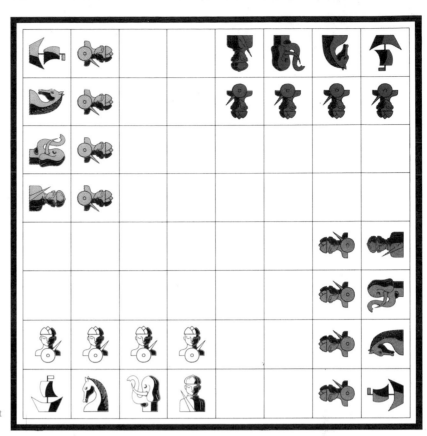

3 Diagram showing the chessboard arranged for the beginning of a game of *chaturanga*, the earliest form of chess, which had four players.

turned up, the king or a pawn must move; if a four, the rook; if a three, the knight; and finally, if a two, the bishop must move. The king could not castle, and a pawn could advance only one step at his first move. These differences apart, the power of the pieces and their moves were very similar to what they are today.

The king moved one step in all directions, the rook, so long as his path was clear, to the four cardinal points, the knight over three squares obliquely, and the bishop moved over two squares diagonally, but the king as well as any other piece could be captured. During play, if one player could bring his king to occupy the square of his allied player's king, the two allied forces united under a single command, and the player whose king's square was occupied dropped out of the game. Unity of command and the two combined forces gave the surviving player an enormous advantage over his two allied adversaries, and greatly enhanced his chances of exterminating the hostile forces under separate commands, with the ultimate object of capturing their king and winning the game.

It is beyond the scope of this work to describe in detail all the moves and ramifications of this ancient Hindu game called *chaturanga,* the origin of which is lost in the depths of remote antiquity. Nevertheless, it survived for some three and a half

2 *(opposite)* Painting on the tomb of Queen Nefertari at Karnak, showing the queen playing chess (or, according to some authorities, draughts).

5

thousand years until the beginning of the sixth century AD. The second (medieval) period began at the start of the sixth century. Considerable changes and improvements were made: the chessboard and power of the pieces remained unaltered, but each pair of allied forces was united under a single command. The two pairs of united forces occupied opposite sides of the chessboard, each united pair controlled by one player who now had sixteen pieces under his command from the beginning of the game. One of the allied kings became a counsellor (or minister) with only half of his original power as an independent king: he now moved only one square diagonally round his monarch. The rook and bishop changed places on the board, the die was discarded, and the game became a trial of mental power and intellectual skill with no element of luck. Each of the two players controlled a king, a counsellor (or minister), two bishops, two knights, two rooks and eight pawns, all occupying exactly the same positions as they do today.

Chess in this form remained unchanged for a thousand years. The third (modern) period opens with the beginning of the sixteenth century. Several important changes were made: the counsellor (or minister) was given the combined power of rook and bishop, the power of the bishop was extended to allow him to command the whole diagonal instead of moving over two

4 *The Game of Chess*, engraving by Sofonisba Anguissola (1555).

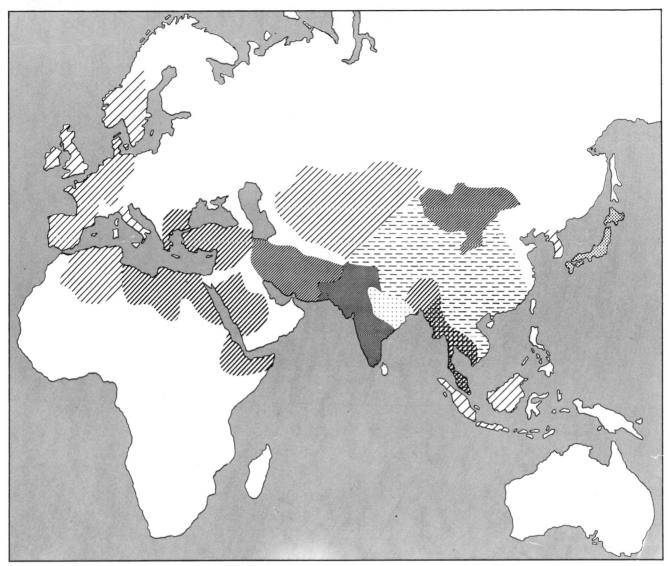

- Chaturanga *2500 BC*
- The Chinese Game (Chong-Ki or Choke-Choo-Hong-Ki) *105 BC*
- The Burmese Game (Chit-Tha-Reen) *600 AD*
- Shogi *1200 AD*
- Shatranj *500 AD*
- Shatranj *6th Century*
- Shatranj *7th Century*
- Shatranj *8th Century*
- Shatranj *later*

5 Map showing the development of the old game of chess throughout the regions of the old world up to 1200 AD.

squares only, the pawns were allowed to advance one or two squares at pleasure on their first move, and finally the king was permitted to castle on either side of the chessboard. The game of chess in this form has remained unaltered until the present time.

In the course of time chess in its medieval form, called *shatranj*, spread throughout India and beyond. Figure 5 shows its progress throughout the regions of the old world.

The game was known throughout India at the beginning of the sixth century, and towards the middle of the century was introduced into Persia and the Byzantine Empire. It reached Medina and Mecca early in the seventh century, and Arabs took the game through Syria, on into North Africa and westward along the North African coast. The Saracens introduced chess into Moorish Spain, and it quickly spread throughout Western Europe, reaching England very early in the tenth century. By the beginning of the twelfth century the Anglo-Normans had introduced it into Ireland.

In the East, the game passed to Mongolia direct from India in the second half of the sixth century, and from there to Outer Mongolia and Russia. In Burma, a modified version of the medieval game, called *chit-tha-reen*, was being played very early in the seventh century; the game had spread there from India, but had been adapted to suit local temperament.

Sumatra received the game from India in its original form, and it spread into Malaya, Java and Borneo. Although the Chinese claim to have invented the game of chess during the Hansing Campaign, in about 105 BC, a careful analysis indicates that their game, which was called *choke-choo-hong-ki*, is a modified version of the Burmese game, itself merely a variation of *shatranj*. It seems probable that the Chinese received the game from India via Tibet, or via Mongolia.

A variation of the medieval game called *shogi* has been played in Japan for at least six hundred years; it is impossible to state with absolute certainty when the game first became known to the Japanese, but it is safe to assume that they received it from Korea during the thirteenth century.

Very few decorative chesspieces associated with a period earlier than the opening of the eighteenth century are known; those that survived have found their rightful places in museums or state collections. Due reference will be made to these important pieces from time to time throughout this work, but for the most part it will be devoted to chesspieces which may at any time be discovered by the diligent collector. The great majority of all beautiful chesspieces were made after the beginning of the eighteenth century, and sets of a type which have come to be known as 'traditional' are, generally, very much later.

6 French copper plaque, dating from the beginning of the nineteenth century, showing a group of people playing or watching a game of chess.

EUROPEAN CHESSPIECES

WITHOUT DOUBT, some beautiful and very important chess sets were made in different parts of Europe at a comparatively early date, but the great majority of all decorative sets were made after the opening of the eighteenth century. The 'Lewis' chesspieces, which are in the British Museum and the Museum of Antiquities in Edinburgh, are the earliest authentic European pieces, but many of the world's museums contain at least a few very early chessmen. The largest and most controversial single piece is the 'Charlemagne King', which is in the Bibliothèque Nationale in Paris. This massive ivory carving portrays an Eastern potentate mounted upon a large elephant with an encircling row of horsemen acting as supporters. Different experts and writers attribute the piece to different periods, from the eighth to sixteenth century, with a number claiming that it is not a chesspiece at all. It carries an Arab (Kufic) inscription which translated reads 'of Yúsuf al-Bahilis' making'.

As has already been mentioned, among the most interesting and important of all early chesspieces are those which have come to be known as the 'Lewis' chessmen. There are seventy-eight, of which sixty-seven are in the British Museum, and the other eleven in the National Museum, Edinburgh. The pieces were found in 1831 in an underground chamber on the west coast of the Isle of Lewis. Their exact origin is unknown; they have been attributed both to Scotland and Scandinavia, since the art of both countries was at that time very similar. They are generally accepted as twelfth century, but could belong to the eleventh; the five pieces shown in figure 7 are carved from morse ivory and are a king, a queen, a knight, a rook and a bishop.

Five medieval chesspieces are to be seen in the Museum of National Antiquities, (Statens Historiska Museum) Stockholm [figure 10]. On the right-hand side is an ivory rook found on the Island of Oland, next comes a thirteenth-century knight, crudely carved from walrus ivory, found at Kalmar Castle, Smaland; next to the knight stands a thirteenth-century bishop carved from walrus ivory, found at Stegeborg Castle, Ostergotland, then a thirteen-century walrus queen found at Vastergotland,

7 *(below and opposite)* Five 'Lewis' chesspieces carved from morse ivory in the eleventh or twelfth century: a king, queen, knight, rook and bishop.

and finally a thirteenth-century walrus rook found in Stockholm. It is possible that the queen and bishop were once part of the same set, but the three other pieces came from totally different sets.

With the exception of the Lewis and kindred pieces, kings and queens of the earliest European sets are roughly shaped throne-like blocks, bishops are cylindrical pieces with two projecting horns, knights are similar in form, but instead of two horns a single projection simulates a horse's head. Rooks are narrow blocks (sometimes tapering from base to top) with channels cut across their tops. Pawns are simple knob- or cone-like pieces, often tapering from base to top with a small ball finial. Even single pieces from such sets are rare, but in the Church of Ager, near Urgel, Catalonia there is an incomplete set, and there are fifteen pieces in the Bischöfliches Diözesanmuseum im Domkreuzgang, Osnabrück.

Few medieval English chesspieces are extant, but in the Salisbury and South Wiltshire Museum is a very beautiful twelfth-century English chess king [figure 9]. This king is carved from walrus ivory, and is probably the earliest authentic English chesspiece known. It has a greenish-grey tinge and this most unusual colouring is probably the outcome of burial.

Silver mounted hardstone chesspieces such as the fourteenth-century St. Louis pieces belonging to the Musée de Cluny are probably the finest of all early sets, but although the quality is not as high, small sets of the fifteenth century made for general use are most interesting and illustrate the evolution of shapes. From about the middle of the fifteenth century chesspieces used for playing were of very simple form and this simplicity persisted, with very few modifications, for four centuries.

FRANCE

For centuries French craftsmen reigned supreme in almost every field of art and this supremacy is clearly reflected in early French chesspieces. The finest sets were the equal of anything produced by master craftsmen working in any country. They are completely individual, well-balanced, perfectly carved or turned, and each piece bears a strict relationship to every other piece in the set both as regards physical dimensions and character. In many of the earlier sets there is an originality entirely foreign to sets made elsewhere. They are outstanding for their great beauty and simplicity. Even modest sets made merely for playing were well designed and perfectly finished.

Craftsmen of every country have a marked tendency to drift to certain districts, and establish themselves into small select colonies. For the most part, French turners and carvers settled in Paris or Dieppe; but scattered throughout the country hundreds of small, single-handed workshops were engaged in the

ivory trade. These small workshops made chess sets on a commercial scale, and in this respect rather overshadowed their English counterparts, where the manufacture of sets was very much a sideline.

African ivory, kiln-dried bone and many types of wood were all used in the production of French chesspieces. One of the finest types of bone sets was that made in and around Dieppe about the middle of the eighteenth century. These quaint and attractive pieces differ in size from set to set, but all are basically similar [figure 8]. The bishops are equipped with felt or leather, silk-fringed hats, and the knights are portrayed as horses' heads with dolphins' tails. All the major pieces of each set are finished in polychrome with silver trim; the pawns' stems and bases (of one side) are pale pink or red, and if complete, the set is housed in a fitted leather box/board. A superior version of this set incorporates bust-type pawns with removable leather hats.

In some similar mid-eighteenth-century sets the pieces were made from African ivory [figure 15]. As will be seen, they have a distinct resemblance to those shown in figure 8; both types are sparsely coloured, and in each case, the opposing pieces are identical, with different colours distinguishing sides. The set shown in figure 15 is sometimes found in bone, but the finish is always the same, and without doubt all were made by the same school of craftsmen working in and about Dieppe. Figure 12 shows a superb eighteenth-century Dieppe chess set carved from African ivory. It was rare for Dieppe sets of this type to be made of ivory.

The lively imagination of French eighteenth-century craftsmen is illustrated in the excellent Dieppe chess set shown in figure 13. It is carved from African ivory and features Frenchmen and Africans. Note the supercilious expressions of the white (French) bishops, and the half-concealed pipe which each is clasping. The knights ride hobby-horses, and a wreath of laurels adorns the hair of each white pawn. The opposing pieces (African) have flat noses, thick lips and woolly hair. Suspecting treachery, the Negro bishops are glancing nervously back over their shoulders. A close study of the pieces reveals that both religious and political satire are reflected in chesspieces of this type.

Apart from those made of bone and ivory there were also many excellent chess sets which were carved and turned from hardwoods [figure 17]. Note the cleft-headed knights; these were made and used from about the middle of the sixteenth century and retained a certain popularity until the close of the eighteenth century. The majority of subsequent imitations were of very poor quality, everyday sets made simply for playing.

During long and arduous coaching journeys, French aristocrats of the eighteenth century often played chess to while away the time. Jostling prevented the use of normal sets and boards, and

11

8 Pieces from a mid-eighteenth-century French chess set carved from bone either in or around Dieppe.

it became customary to use a cushion chessboard with spiked chesspieces. The cushion was suitably embroidered with squares to form a chessboard, and the chesspieces terminated in tapering spikes. Figure 11 shows pieces belonging to an exquisitely carved African ivory cushion set. Beautiful and delicate pieces such as these must not be confused with similar, but crudely carved, pieces made from ivory or bone exclusively for play upon a chessboard scratched in sand. Beach play was very popular in French watering-places, and many spiked chess sets were in use at this time.

In the second half of the eighteenth century, charming little chesspieces carved from African ivory and finished in polychrome were produced in quantities; they are well carved and carefully painted, but obviously made as a commercial proposition [figure 16]. Similar sets incorporating domed rooks and smaller pawns were made in Germany; the German versions were made in the first half of the nineteenth century, and are always unpainted.

Figure 18 shows pieces of a type produced from ivory, wood and bone for at least two hundred years. Exclusively French,

9 Twelfth-century king carved in England from walrus ivory (probably the earliest authentic English chesspiece known).

they have *fou* heads as finials to the bishops. The set illustrated is the best of this particular type, and is perfectly turned and carved, with a very high finish. Other sets of this type were made cheaply for play or export; they were made from softwoods and lack the high degree of finish possible with hardwoods.

Superb chesspieces portraying the struggle between England and France towards the close of the eighteenth century were carved in Paris and Dieppe throughout the first half of the nineteenth century [figure 19]. The pieces shown were carved from African ivory in Dieppe during the first quarter of the nineteenth century and are polychromed throughout. Napoleon and Josephine are featured as the French king and queen with Marshals Ney and Massena as bishops. The knights are French dragoons, and Napoleon's Old Guard are pawns. The French *columbs* have eagle surmounts. The opposing king and queen portray George III and Queen Charlotte; Lord Nelson and the Duke of Wellington are bishops, the knights are British dragoons, and the pawns, British grenadiers.

For many years this chess set occupied the chess table on which Napoleon played many games in the Café de la Régence 13

10 *(above and below)* Five medieval ivory chesspieces found in Sweden.

11 Six pieces from a French cushion set made in the eighteenth century.

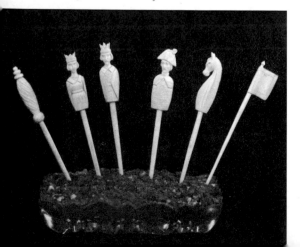

in Paris. The table still exists, and is preserved with considerable reverence. It carries the inscription '*Table sur laquelle Bonaparte le Consul jouait aux échecs au Café de la Régence en 1798*'. Stories concerning Napoleon's prowess as a chess player are many and varied; if we bear in mind his exceptional mental power in other directions, we must come to the conclusion that he was a player of no mean order. These particular chesspieces are reputed to have belonged to the Emperor himself.

In spite of the confusion of periods, many 'bust' type chesspieces, carved in and around Paris, portray Napoleon and Henri IV as rival kings [figure 21]. Boldly, but beautifully, carved from African ivory with the pieces of one side stained crimson, this and many similar sets were made in the first half of the nineteenth century on a commercial basis.

Another set with similar characteristics has as a theme the Battle of Waterloo. In this set, Napoleon is featured as the red king, with Josephine as his queen; Marshals Berthier and Massena are his bishops, Napoleon's Old Guard are pawns and the knights are fiery French chargers. The Duke of Wellington is the white king, the Duchess of Wellington is queen, Lords Liverpool and Castlereagh are bishops and the pawns are British grenadiers.

The great versatility and fertile imagination of French nineteenth-century craftsmen are at once apparent when we look at figures 20, 14 and 29. In the first of these Louis XIV features as a king; in the second the Canadian campaign of 1759-60 is portrayed, with North-American Indians featured as knights and pawns (rarely does one find North-American Indians portrayed in chesspieces of any origin); and in the last we see the legends of Ancient Egypt. Well carved and finely painted chess sets such as these were made from African ivory in both Paris and Dieppe. Other equally spectacular sets feature battle scenes, pages from history, and often portray members of the British, Dutch, French or German monarchy. All such sets were made by two small schools of craftsmen.

In France few important chess sets were made from silver; they were costly to produce, and demand was small. Figure 28 shows one of the very few silver sets of French origin known. Each piece carries the Paris silver mark for 1819. The whole set is well chased throughout, with the pieces of one side finished in silver gilt. Other silver sets were certainly made in France, but they are difficult to locate, and doubtful sets carry no marks.

Early in the nineteenth century, the old established works at Rouen made a quantity of singularly attractive faience 'St George' type chesspieces complete with matching 'tray' chessboards. They were well potted and painted in brilliant colours – all heavily glazed. It will be seen that the *fleur-de-lys* is repeated again and again in the arabesque design, and that the reds, blues,

12 *(above and below)* Superb French chesspieces made in Dieppe from African ivory about the middle of the eighteenth century.

13 African ivory pieces carved in Dieppe towards the end of the eighteenth century.

greens and yellows all blend in perfect harmony [figure 34]. 'St George' type chesspieces were made and used for over two centuries throughout Europe. Being of simple form, the pieces were easy to turn, and there was no difficulty in using cheap woods for such robust shapes. Another very important point was that there was little risk of confusion during actual play. Until superseded by the 'Staunton' midway through the nineteenth century, the 'St George' was probably the most popular of all playing pieces. One delightful modern set is made entirely from shells [figure 35]; it is included to illustrate the enormous variety of materials used in the manufacture of chesspieces. Craftsmen throughout the ages have fashioned chesspieces from every imaginable substance and the search for new materials continues today with the emphasis on stainless steel and plastics.

ENGLAND

With the exception of anything made to special order, fine chesspieces were not carved in England until the middle of the nineteenth century. Even at that late date very few were made, but from the beginning of the century quantities of turned sets were produced. A very different set of circumstances from those in France existed in England; in France, cheap sets were made on a commercial basis for export to England, and these satisfied local English demands, so that the making of chess sets

15

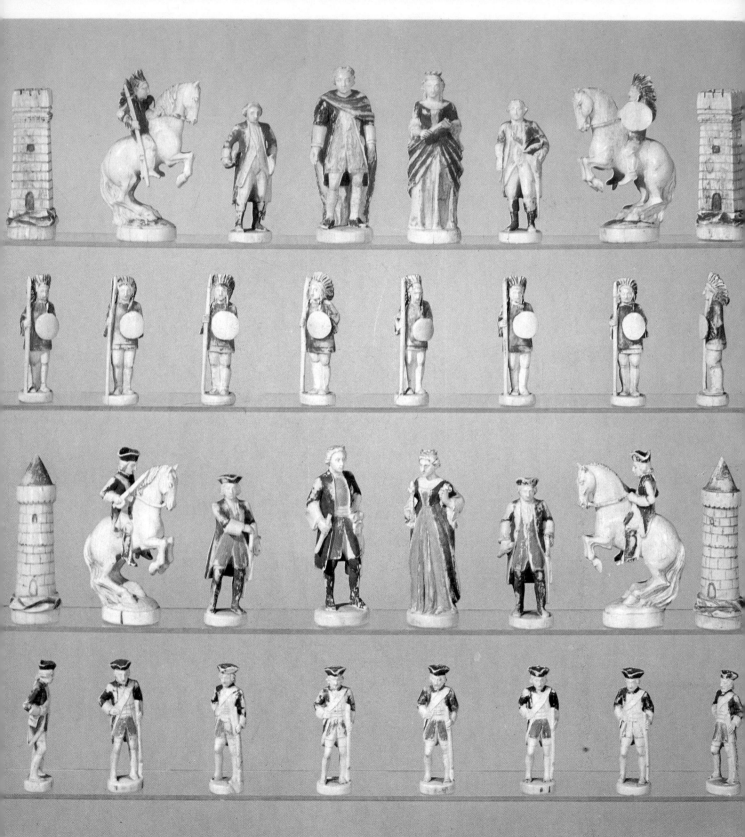

14 (left) Early nineteenth-century pieces carved in Paris from African ivory and finished in polychrome.

15 (above right) The pieces of one side of an African ivory set made in Dieppe in 1750.

16 (below right) One of the well-carved and painted sets made commercially in France from African ivory in the second half of the eighteenth century.

17 French hardwood pieces made in the eighteenth century including the cleft-headed knight which had been in use since the beginning of the sixteenth century.

18 French ivory or hardwood pieces made early in the nineteenth century and incorporating 'fou' heads.

was regarded merely as a sideline. The bulk of all English turning was done on piecework rates by single-handed turners slaving away in small workshops scattered about London and Birmingham. As and when required, a miscellaneous assortment of work was turned for the ivory trade. Ivory engraving, or chasing as it was then termed, constituted an entirely separate branch of the trade, and almost all ivory chasers worked in and around Sheffield.

Primarily to indicate that it was of English manufacture, many of the leading firms engaged in the ivory trade marked their merchandise; well-established firms such as Calvert, Lund, Pringle and Toy had their names and places of business engraved on the bases of the chesspieces they sold. The very high standard set by nineteenth-century English chasers can be seen in the quality of this engraving.

A large number of different types of English chess sets appeared during the first half of the nineteenth century. Derivatives of these basic types are legion, which is not altogether surprising since, as already stated, the turning of chesspieces was merely a sideline among English turners, who worked to no absolute standards. There was the Old English 'Barlycorn', so called because of the corn leaves and husks engraved and carved on the main pieces [figure 22]; 'Uprights', another type once very popular in the North of England [figure 23]; and the misnamed 'Maltese' [figure 24]. Some very fine sets were made by Messrs Calvert of Fleet Street [figure 32].

Toy Bros of London produced some beautiful turned sets. They are heavy but well-balanced and, although decorative, do not suffer from over-elaboration. The best English chesspieces made during the nineteenth century came from the workshop of Charles Hastilow [figure 25]; one of his finest sets was displayed, complete with matching chessboard, in the Great Exhibition of 1851.

In the field of ceramics, and more especially pottery, England more than held her own. Josiah Wedgwood, the master of all potters, produced outstanding chesspieces from the models of John Flaxman towards the end of the eighteenth century. Among collectors, Wedgwood chesspieces are probably the most desirable of all pottery pieces; they were produced in the Etruria works, which are located some two miles from Burslem in Staffordshire. The earliest pieces were fired in November 1763. At the outset, three different kings and three different queens were made. There wer two types of bishop, but only one type of rook and knight. Charles Kemble, brother of Sarah Siddons, the greatest tragic actress of her time, sat as model for the kings and Mrs Siddons herself sat for the queens. One type of bishop was a mitred figure with upraised arm, the other a jester or French fou. The fou bishops were for sets destined for the French market.

(following spread)

19 *(left)* The king and queen (Napoleon and Josephine) from a nineteenth-century French set carved in African ivory.

20 *(right)* Pieces from a French African ivory set produced in the early nineteenth century; Louis XIV is depicted as king.

21 *(above and below)* The rival kings in this French 'bust' type set made of African ivory depict Napoleon and Henri IV, a frequent combination in nineteenth-century sets, in spite of the obvious anachronism.

The rooks were tapering square castellated towers with elevated turrets. Complete sets are beautifully moulded, well finished, and perfectly balanced [figure 36].

Rough mounds served as bases for the very earliest pieces, later giving way to scalloped plinths and double octagonal stands. It is important to appreciate that, quite apart from their quality and beauty, Wedgwood chesspieces were the first portrait sets to be produced in pottery. Few of the original sets have survived, but in 1926 the original moulds were recovered and restored, and used once again to produce beautiful chesspieces of similar quality.

The earliest mark was the well known 'WEDGWOOD', sometimes with initials; Flaxman's model numbers also often appear, scratched in the paste. A great variety of attractive colours used for the older pieces included mauve, light brown, blue, green, buff and white. The pieces of one side were sometimes one colour throughout; sometimes the two colours forming one complete set would be mounted upon bases of white pottery, but more usually the actual pieces would be white and the bases coloured (one colour for each side). In some very early sets boxwood and ebony plinths were used to distinguish sides.

The small Castleford establishment twelve miles from Leeds made quantities of small military-style chesspieces from pottery at the beginning of the nineteenth century. These small pieces were fairly well potted, but not too well finished. Various colours were used – cream and brown, cream and green, cream and black, cream and blue.

At Swinton, near Rotherham, Yorkshire, on the estate of the Marquis of Rockingham, a small pottery was established in 1757. There are some unique chesspieces in the Yorkshire Museum, York, which have been attributed to Swinton, but there is considerable doubt about their exact origin. Only six pieces exist, none of which are marked, so until other pieces from a similar set are discovered their origin will remain uncertain. Meanwhile it is fairly safe to assume that these important pieces are not Swinton, but either Derby or Staffordshire [figure 30].

Soon after the beginning of the nineteenth century, the pottery passed into the hands of John and William Brameld. The works were enlarged and only the finest quality ceramics produced. Towards the close of the first quarter of the century, a few delightful chess sets were produced in porcelain which compare favourably with the best porcelain sets made anywhere. The pieces closely resemble earlier Meissen pieces, but were not exact copies. The form is similar, but they were painted in the exclusive apple green and periwinkle blue of Rockingham.

In the final quarter of the nineteenth century, while working in the great Doulton establishment, the well-known pottery designer George Tinworth created a few very interesting chess

19

22, 23, 24, 25 Pieces from
four sets made in England in the early
nineteenth century. *(top to bottom)*
'Barlycorn' pieces in bone; 'Uprights'
turned from bone; pieces turned from
ivory and of the type often misnamed
'Maltese'; ivory pieces made by Charles
Hastilow.

sets. Each piece was a mouse; the sides were identical in form,
but one was coloured deep brown, the other a light straw, or
brownish-yellow; the colour differs from set to set. Each mouse
carried Tinworth's monogram, impressed at the rear. They were
finished in very heavy glaze. These interesting little pottery sets
were not produced in any quantity, and today are most difficult
to find.

Perhaps the most appealing ceramic set ever produced was
made in the celebrated Minton works in Stoke-on-Trent. The
beautiful pieces were made from Parian ware. Some sets were
painted in natural colours and finished in gilt [figure 37], but
similar sets were finished in self colours only and these were
left unglazed. Unglazed sets are found in white and green, white
and blue, or white and chocolate. Some sets will be found unmarked, but others carry the impressed (Minton) mark. The
exact date is obscure, but Parian ware was only perfected in
1842, so it is probably that they were made in the latter part of
that century.

English chesspieces in silver are very rare, and they were
never produced as a commercial proposition. None were made
before the nineteenth century, and even then, the only sets
made were specially commissioned, or made as examples of the
silversmith's art. Figure 31 shows a fine set made by E. Fennel,
which carries the English silver mark for 1815. Both sides are
identical, but one is gold-plated.

Throughout its history, nothing has made such an impact on

chess design as the introduction of English Staunton chesspieces.
The Staunton set was designed by Nathaniel Cook in 1835 at a
time when players were refusing to play with each other's pieces
because of the difficulty in distinguishing the various pieces
which made up English, Dublin and Edinburgh sets. With the
object of preventing confusion during play, the designer used
symbols in their plainest form – for the king, a crown; for the
queen, a coronet; for the bishop, a mitre; for the knight, a horse's
head; for the rook, a castle; and for the pawn, a ball. The horses'
heads were based on the Elgin Marbles, and the pawns were
developed from the freemason's square and compass. Every
symbol was supported on a plain, elegant stem rising from a
heavy, wide base which gave complete stability. The design
made such an impression on the original John Jaques, principal
of the great manufacturing works bearing his name, that he
immediately suggested making it on a commercial basis.

The designer was a friend of the English master player,
Howard Staunton, who sanctioned the request that the design
be called 'Staunton chessmen'. Mr Jaques obtained a copyright
for the design, and began manufacturing the set in his Leather
Lane, London, EC 1, establishment. Later the factory was moved
to No. 102, Hatton Garden, London, EC 1 where Staunton chessmen continued to be made until the Second World War. By kind
permission of John Jaques (present head of the firm) figure 26
shows a unique photograph of the original Staunton chesspieces
in the first pattern book. Unfortunately, fire damaged the pattern
book, but the essential features are perfectly clear.

Over a long period, many thousands of Staunton chess sets
were made from wood and ivory. The wooden pieces were turned
from ebony and boxwood and very heavily weighted. Only the
finest quality African ivory was used for the ivory sets. Both
types of set were made in several sizes, but the most popular size
for general play was the $3\frac{1}{2}$-inch. For match or tournament games
the $4\frac{1}{2}$-inch was preferred.

For actual play, Staunton chesspieces stand supreme; never
has the type been equalled and, over the years, it has established
itself as the absolute standard. Every piece bears a direct relation-

28 (opposite) Two pieces from one of the rare French silver chess sets. They bear the Paris silver mark of 1819.

ship to its name; the king's side rooks and knights are marked with a small crown to enable a player to see at once which is which, irrespective of the position it occupies on the chessboard.

Unfortunately the war put an end to the manufacture of these perfect playing sets, but in the new Thornton Heath factory in Surrey, John Jaques & Son, Ltd, the sole producers of the original Staunton chesspieces, now make the 3½-inch size. Figure 27 shows one half of an original Staunton chess set in ivory (apart from colour, both sides are alike), and figure 33 is a close-up of a Staunton knight showing the small crown engraved upon the king's side knights and rooks.

During the First World War many chess sets were improvised for actual use and, soon after the war had finished, sets made from cartridge cases were made as souvenirs. The set in figure 117 is made from standard thirty-calibre cartridge cases used in Springfield rifles; it is well made and superior to most similar sets. Some have small wooden symbols fitted into open-ended cases, others have the bullet end flattened and cut to shape.

29 Pieces from a French African ivory set carved in the middle of the nineteenth century.

GERMANY

For sheer excellence and beauty, the finest examples of chess-pieces produced by early German craftsmen have rarely been equalled and never surpassed. It is clear that much thought was given to the subject portrayed, to its design, and to its historic association. Right down to the smallest detail everything is meticulously correct. African ivory, bone, hardwoods, gold, silver, amber, hardstones, brass and iron were all used to great effect. Craftsmen working in the regions of Augsburg or Nuremberg were mainly responsible, but numbers of fine sets were made in other parts of Germany.

Hardwood sets of great beauty sometimes had silver mounts which invariably carry Nuremberg silver marks; this does not exclude the possibility that the pieces were carved elsewhere, then mounted by Nuremberg silversmiths.

Woodcarvers working in the Tyrol and Black Forest areas made chesspieces to a multiplicity of designs; these sets were boldly carved from a variety of different woods. They show

30 *(above and below)* Unique English ceramic chesspieces, probably Derby or Staffordshire, which can now be seen in the Yorkshire Museum.

an abundance of imagination, but lack refinement. Figure 38 shows a carved hardwood and African ivory set made somewhere in South Germany early in the eighteenth century; it enjoys a charm altogether lacking in more sophisticated sets made at a later date in the same area. Several unrelated features are evident in the set: helmets worn by the white side closely resemble those portrayed in Danish pieces of later origin, and the black side turbans have much in common with those worn in North Africa and Turkey. The castles carried by the elephant rooks savour of French *Directoire* pieces, but the knight, both in type and posture, is without question South German.

Every piece comprising the exquisite set shown in figure 39 is meticulously carved from amber of differing colours. It was made during the second half of the eighteenth century in South Germany. The silver mounts are unmarked. Carved from African ivory in the third quarter of the eighteenth century, figure 40 shows a beautiful set made in Nuremberg. Sets of this general type, all with impeccable finish, were carved in Nuremberg and Augsburg. Almost always, the eyes of the pieces were made prominent by piercing and colouring the pupils. Hardwood sets of similar type had the pupils burnt in. In common with many German sets this example has identical sides.

Figure 44 shows a large German chess set carved from African ivory to a Gothic theme in the first half of the nineteenth century. German sets such as this always excel in facial carving and precise attention to detail; this attention to detail is evident in the bases of the knights, which are lifelike representations of castles. Nevertheless, the general finish of this and other large sets made in Germany falls below the standard set by French craftsmen of the same period.

'Reynard the Fox' chesspieces, carved to the designs produced by von Kaulbach for Goethe's translations, are most rare [figure 43]. The set shown here is brilliantly carved from African ivory, and is probably the finest example known. Reynard is featured in the four bishops with lions and lionesses as kings and queens. There is, in the old Historisches Stadt-Museum in Munich, a somewhat similar set attributed to von Kaulbach himself, but it does not equal in quality the set shown here. Earlier Reynard the Fox sets made in the second half of the eighteenth century have monkey pawns, but here each pawn is a different animal – monkey, bird or rodent.

It is not uncommon to find early German chess sets in which the two sides are carved from different substances. Figure 42 shows part of an important German set carved in the last quarter of the eighteenth century from amber and African ivory. The amber side portrays Catherine de' Medici with her followers; carved from ivory, the Huguenots under Condé are the opposing forces. It is more than possible that the Battle of Jarnac (1569),

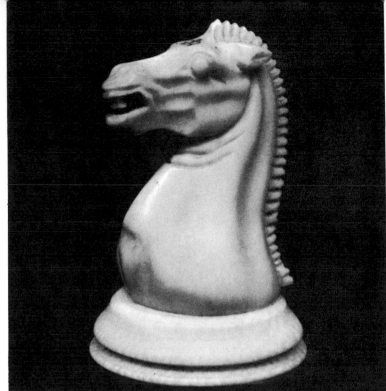

31 This knight, carved from the design seen in figure 26, shows the small crown engraved on king's side knights and rooks for identification.

32 Silver pieces made by the English designer E. Fennel in 1815.

33 Ivory chesspieces made in the nineteenth century and marketed by Messrs Calvert of Fleet Street in London.

when the Huguenots were defeated and Condé slain, inspired this beautiful set. Another amber set, made in North Germany, is shown in figure 53. It is complete with the original chessboard.

Very fine and important chesspieces were made from porcelain during the eighteenth century by the celebrated factories of Meissen and Frankenthal. Superbly moulded from the finest quality porcelain, and beautifully painted, these exquisite chesspieces stand alone.

The Meissen porcelain set in figure 120 is of the finest quality porcelain and delightfully painted. Established at Meissen on the Elbe, near Dresden, under the auspices of Augustus II, Elector of Saxony and King of Poland, early in the eighteenth century, the Meissen porcelain works has, from time to time throughout its history, produced several types of fine chesspieces, but sets made after the close of the eighteenth century lack the subtle charm of earlier pieces. The set illustrated was made in 1745. Later sets are well finished but painted in brighter colours with a fair amount of gilding, whereas the very early sets are without

34 *(opposite above)* Faïence pieces of the 'St George' type, made in Rouen in the early nineteenth century.

35 *(opposite below)* Contemporary French pieces made entirely from shells.

36 *(above)* Wedgwood pottery pieces made in the Etruria works from Flaxman's models towards the end of the eighteenth century.

37 *(above right)* Nineteenth-century Minton ceramic pieces.

gilding. The factory continues to make fine porcelain chess sets; Professor Max Esser of Berlin designed the modern 'marine' set, and other well-known designers have been responsible for different, but less familiar types. Figure 45 shows a modern set believed to have been designed by Struck in which each piece is a frog. It is beautifully made throughout and, although modern, is far from common. In the early part of the nineteenth century, good porcelain chesspieces were produced in other factories. Fürstenberg, Ludwigsburg and Volkstadt all made fine sets. Figure 55, for instance, shows a fine set made in the Fürstenberg porcelain factory established by Charles, Duke of Brunswick, in 1750 under the direction of Benckgraff, late of the Höchst

38 Pieces from a carved hardwood and ivory set made in South Germany in the early eighteenth century.

establishment. Fine quality ware after the style of Meissen was produced, and for a factory mark, the letter 'F', usually in blue, was used. The pieces are of excellent quality throughout, and are usually finished in white and bistre with gold trim. Almost identical sets were made at Volkstadt, located in the forest region of Thuringia. They were finished in white and pale blue, marked with the symbol of a hayfork (for Rudolfstadt) or the letters 'cv' (for Volkstadt).

Another very important German porcelain chess set owes its origin to the factory of Ludwigsburg, located near Stuttgart [figure 54]. Heinrich der Löwe riding a lion is portrayed as king, with jesters mounted upon asses as his bishops. Each piece is marked with a double c, which was the factory mark for 1806 to 1818. Sets from the same moulds were finished in two colours – white and green.

Irrespective of the process which was employed in their manufacture, silver chess sets were always costly to produce, and never enjoyed the popularity of well-carved ivory or wooden pieces. Apart from the few eighteenth-century silver sets made

39 Amber chesspieces on silver bases; a set made in South Germany in the later eighteenth century.

in Augsburg or Nuremberg, at least one elaborate set was made in Königsberg, in East Prussia, in 1778. It featured a battle between Roman and Moorish forces, and is complete with a silver chessboard. It was once in the possession of Baron von Minnegerode of Rossitten. Perhaps the oldest of all German silver chess sets is one that was made in Nuremberg in about 1700.

Rarely does one find two totally different metals constituting one set of chesspieces, but one German nineteenth-century set [figure 50] has silver figures on one (the German) side, and bronze on the other (Russian). The set is unmarked, and it was probably made by an Austrian craftsman working in or near Augsburg; it certainly has a German origin.

40 African ivory pieces; Nuremberg, eighteenth century.

41 English nineteenth-century chesspieces
turned from African ivory.

As a medium from which to make low-priced decorative chess-pieces in metal, cast-iron was an obvious choice; as long as the original models from which the moulds were taken were the work of a highly skilled craftsman, ornamental sets of great merit could be cast very cheaply. The best cast-iron pieces were designed and made at Hanau by Zimmerman, who cast no fewer than eight totally different types in his foundry just east of Frankfurt. Many of Zimmerman's best sets are found to be stamped with the name and the pattern number; other identical sets carry no marks whatsoever. The set shown in figure 46 was cast about the middle of the nineteenth century and is the most famous of all Zimmerman's products. It is similar in design to the set presented to the great American chess player, Paul Morphy, after his return to American from London.

Paul Morphy was born on 22 June 1837 in the city of New Orleans. After an elementary education at the Jefferson Academy, he proceeded to a college near Mobile, Alabama. He graduated from there in 1854, and quickly established himself as a chess player of genius. Having triumphed over all American opposition, he decided to visit England, where, he had been assured, he would find antagonists who were more than his match. In June 1858 he arrived in London, and after a few preliminary setbacks, soon established himself, and dispelled any doubts regarding his supremacy as a player. Having en-encountered and defeated all the noted players of his day, with the sole exception of one with whom he could not obtain a meeting, Paul Morphy returned to America, where he received a hero's welcome. On 25 May 1859, a magnificent gold and silver chess set was presented to him in the chapel of New York University as a mark of esteem, and as a testimonial to the success of his European tour, during which he had established himself

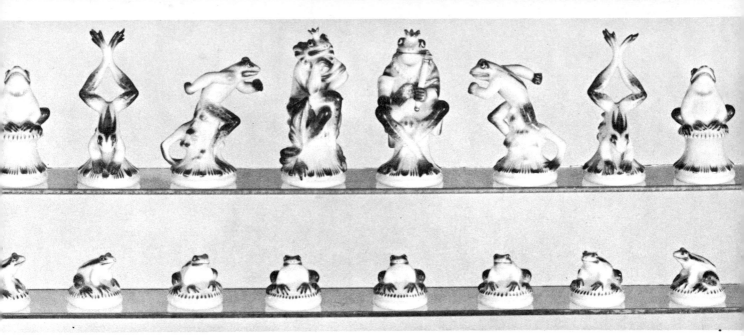

45 Twentieth-century Meissen pieces.

46 Cast-iron pieces of the Morphy type, made by Zimmerman in nineteenth-century Germany.

as a player without equal, and a perfect gentleman. It is generally accepted that cast-iron sets of the type shown [figure 46] are reproductions of the pieces presented to Paul Morphy, but it is much more likely that both the presentation set, and those produced by Zimmerman, were copies taken from much earlier pieces of German origin. (Chesspieces of exactly the same type were produced in Spain from brass.)

Many other, but little known, foundries throughout Germany made interesting small chesspieces. No maker's mark was used, and it is probable that most of the unmarked 'Zimmerman Sets' were cast by one of these foundries after making moulds from Zimmerman pieces.

ITALY

Working in the sixteenth and seventeenth centuries, craftsmen of Milan and Florence are reputed to have carved incredibly beautiful chesspieces. Without doubt several important sets were produced by these early Milanese and Florentine craftsmen. However, since each set was made to special commission or command, it is doubtful if such pieces, even if they have survived, will be found by collectors. The inventories of prominent fifteenth- and sixteenth-century figures often listed chesspieces. It can be stated with certainty that the vast majority of all playing chesspieces have, at all times, been of simple form. An inspection of early paintings and prints will serve to prove the point.

Figure 47 shows a beautiful Florentine chess set turned and carved from African ivory in the third quarter of the eighteenth century. Both sides are identical, but one is stained pale green. Roman emperors and empresses are portrayed as the kings and

35

47 African ivory pieces carved in Italy in the
late eighteenth century.

48 African ivory pieces carved at the beginning of the nineteenth century in Italy.

queens, Roman officials symbolize the bishops, the knights are bridled horses' heads, and the rooks are castellated towers. The well-turned pawns are simple stems terminating in acorn finials. The excellence of early Italian craftsmanship is evident throughout this charming set and the one shown in figure 48, which again features Roman emperors and empresses as the kings and queens.

Towards the close of the eighteenth century, highly imaginative chesspieces were carved by Italian craftsmen. Human beings, fish, insects, and birds were all used as themes. The quality is always high, and the workmanship is altogether distinctive. Amusing zoomorphic and piscatorial sets [figure 49] were carved from African ivory in Italy and Germany. Sometimes there is confusion in attributing these sets to either Germany or Italy, but, generally speaking, German sets are larger, with less attention to detail.

Early Italian silver sets are unmarked, and although a careful examination of any silver chess set will supply some indication of origin, in most cases the final decision is little better than a shrewd guess based upon style and workmanship.

Working in glass, Venetian craftsmen of the nineteenth century produced a variety of chesspieces. Like glass sets made in France, they were based upon earlier ivory or porcelain sets. Some were blown from clear or coloured crystal, others, much more complex in structure, could only have been made by master craftsmen. The more decorative and complex types were indeed difficult to make; they were made from solid crystal of several different colours fused together, formed to the desired shape on the pontil rod, and finally overlaid. The several elements entering into the complex structure of these pieces necessitated a comprehensive knowledge of annealing, since otherwise cracking would have been inevitable.

49 Italian piscatorial pieces carved from African ivory in the nineteenth century.

50 *(above and below)* Silver and bronze pieces from a nineteenth-century German set.

Simple 'St George' type chesspieces were made from very hard glass early in the nineteenth century; they originated in Venice and are found in several colours: clear and pale green, clear and yellow, clear and blue, and clear and mauve. Other Venetian sets were blown from soft glass, and were hollow with corks at their bases. They were intended to be filled with coloured liquids; when filled such sets were very decorative, but they proved to be quite impractical.

CENTRAL EUROPE

From the second quarter of the eighteenth, and throughout the entire nineteenth century, craftsmen of Austria and Hungary carved beautiful chesspieces in their homelands; at the same time, migratory Austrians and Hungarians were responsible for some of the finest sets attributed to other European countries. The chesspieces produced followed no particular style; each set was made to an individual design, and reflected the craftsman's ability. Austrian and Hungarian chesspieces carved in the eighteenth century from ivory or hardwood leave nothing to be desired, but throughout the succeeding century, thousands of sets were carved from softwoods. They were cut to a multiplicity of designs; animals, birds, tradesmen and peasantry were all used as themes, and although the craftsmanship was quite commendable, the overall quality did not approach the immaculate perfection of the earlier work. Eighteenth-century hardwood sets sometimes incorporated refined editions of the double-headed horses so often used to illustrate knights in very early chess literature. Figure 52 shows an eighteenth-century Austrian chess set of this type; kindred pieces of German origin often have human faces carved on the body of the kings, queens and bishops.

Figure 60 shows a very rare Austro-Hungarian glass chess set of the Biedermeier period. The light side is made of what is now

39

51 Italian eighteenth-century chesspieces carved from African ivory.

52 Pieces from one side of an Austrian set made of hardwood; note the double-headed knights.

known as uranium glass, the opposing pieces of glass containing a percentage of gold oxide. The faces and finials of this set are most carefully painted, and the whole set is finished in gilt trim.

The few silver chess sets made by eighteenth-century Austrian and Hungarian craftsmen carry no mark, so it is impossible to state their exact date of manufacture and precise origin. Many have been attributed to Germany and to other European countries. During the first quarter of the twentieth century, a few very elaborate sets were made from silver [figures 62 and 56]. The set illustrated is complete with matching chessboard, and is a masterpiece of the silversmith's art. The pieces are made of solid silver and are encrusted with precious stones: amethyst, turquoise, cornelian and topaz. Some of the larger stones have *intaglio* engravings, and the matching chessboard, which is also of silver, carries many fired enamel heraldic arms and emblems. Figure 56 shows one of the chesspieces, and clearly illustrates the high degree of finish and general quality – it will be seen that one side is finished in gold plate. (A current edition of this set is now made in Hungary, but there is a very real difference in quality. On the set shown, all the detail is beautifully tooled and chased, whereas the tooling and chasing is absent in the new sets, which rely on enamelling to highlight details.) Fine quality chesspieces made from brass, bronze and pewter can with certainty be attributed to Hungary, but they carry no maker's marks.

53 Amber chesspieces on an amber board made in North Germany in the eighteenth century.

In the second half of the nineteenth century dainty little porcelain chesspieces were produced in the Viennese Imperial China Establishment. One type only was made; faultlessly moulded, it was skilfully, but sparsely, painted in yellow and black with a gilt finish. After a lapse in manufacture, an almost identical set was produced in 1926, and again in the post-war years. The quality of paste and moulding is identical, but the original embellishment is somewhat superior.

Chesspieces unique in design were produced by ivory and bone turners working in the twin states of Bosnia and Herzegovina towards the end of the eighteenth century. Kings, queens, bishops and pawns were all symbolized by carved human heads mounted upon pear-shaped stems rising from carved circular bases. The knights were fore-parts of bridled horses, and the rooks were pear-shaped castellated towers. Bosnian chesspieces can hardly be called beautiful, but they possess great appeal, and are extremely rare.

Woodcarving reached near perfection in parts of Bohemia about the close of the eighteenth century; the pieces in figure 57 were carved in the nineteenth century. Wood-turning during the early part of the nineteenth century equalled the wood-carving in perfection, as can be seen in figure 58, which shows a well-carved early nineteenth-century chess set made from hardwood. Many similar sets were made throughout Central

43

55 *(opposite)* German porcelain pieces made in the Fürstenberg factory in the early nineteenth century.

Europe during the early part of the century; some were simply turned, others incorporated symbols representing busts or human heads, but in each set the knights were double-headed horses.

For a very long time good quality glass sets have been manufactured in Czechoslovakia. Few of the earlier sets have survived, but over the last fifty years or so, fine heavy sets have been made from clear and black glass. The kings, queens, bishops and pawns are reproductions of Roman busts, the knights fine,

54 Porcelain pieces made in the Ludwigsburg factory in Germany in the early nineteenth century.

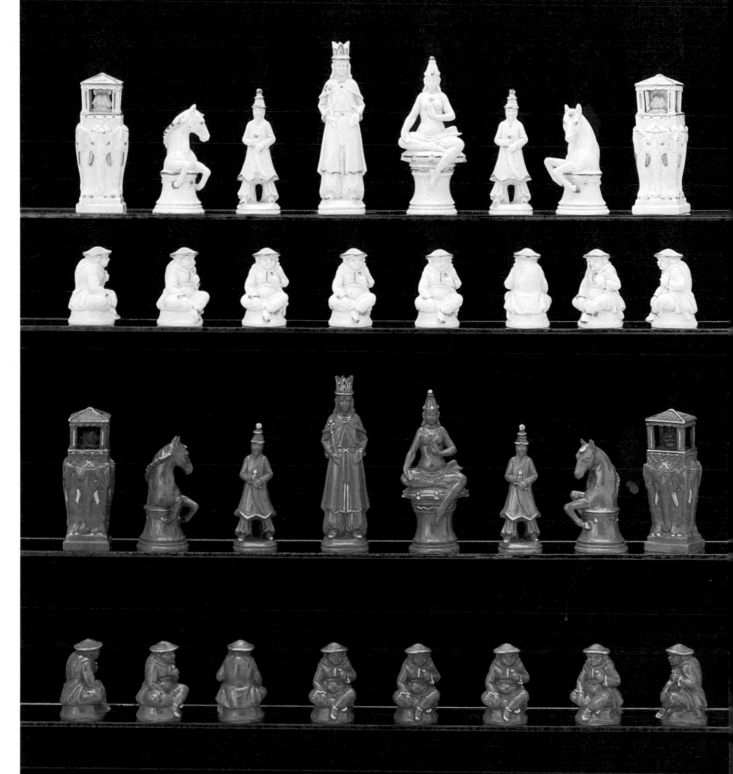

56 A gold-plated solid silver pawn from the set seen in figure 62.

57 Hardwood pieces carved in Bohemia in the nineteenth century; note the double-headed knights also found in figure 52.

bold horses' heads, and the rooks heavy towers. The earlier versions carry a raised butterfly mark.

Rumania and Bulgaria produced cheap painted wooden sets which are interesting and attractive, but deficient in quality and general finish.

Swiss nineteenth-century carvers produced quantities of soft-wood chess sets; the best attained a very high standard, but the majority were made on a commercial basis by craftsmen normally engaged in other branches of the woodcarving industry. Probably the most popular theme used was the 'bears of Berne' [figure 59]. Birds and animals were also a great favourite with Swiss carvers. A few very fine sets were also carved from African ivory by early nineteenth-century Swiss craftsmen; these again used the 'bears of Berne' theme, and compare quite favourably with the best French and German sets of the same period. It is probable that they were all made by one small school of carvers, the same school which carved the finest quality wooden sets.

NORTHERN EUROPE

Chesspieces made by early Danish craftsmen are always of a very high standard. Only the very best quality ivory was used and this careful selection is clearly apparent in the exceptional finish of their sets. Perhaps the earliest known Danish chesspieces are the sixteenth-century pieces to be seen in the National-museet, Copenhagen [figure 61]. The central figure is a king, which was found before 1869 at Vordingborg, Zealand; to his right stands a queen found before 1841 near Randers, Jutland; and to his left stands a rook found before 1856 at Frederiksberg, Copenhagen.

In Holland large quantities of playing sets were turned from ivory, bone and wood; the best equalled the better quality French and German sets of a similar type. From the middle of of the eighteenth century many versions of the same basic design were turned from ivory and bone. Many of these sets are spindly by today's standards, but they are quite well balanced, and were ideally suited to the small squares found on early chessboards and tables.

Silver chesspieces were produced by both Danish and Dutch silversmiths; the sets produced were well designed and carefully finished, but did not compare with the early German silver sets. There is one fine Dutch silver set in which Gustavus Adolphus and Ferdinand of Austria are portrayed; these delightful little pieces have an aura of swashbuckling gaiety seldom encountered in silver chess sets. Each piece is impressed with the Dutch silvermark for 1860. An almost identical set was cast by Zimmerman [figure 122].

Most unusual themes are encountered in early Flemish chesspieces. Figure 121 shows a rare and important set portraying

58 Pearwood pieces from one of the finest sets carved in Bohemia in the early nineteenth century.

59 Pearwood set carved in Switzerland in the nineteenth century and showing the 'bears of Berne'.

Swiss and Austrian sides. In this particular set, which is well carved from African ivory, galleys represent the rooks; normally in sets of this type the rooks arc Swiss chalets. Eighteenth-century Flemish craftsmen were among the world's best carvers. They excelled in the manufacture of groups, cups, plaques and tankards, but the carving of chesspieces was not regarded as a serious occupation. Nevertheless, the few sets they produced are of very high quality.

'Virtue versus vice' was a popular theme in the early nineteenth century. The white king and queen are attended by two court officials holding closed Bibles, knights are mounted pages and the pawns cherubs carrying different love emblems. Mephistopheles, the red king, and his semi-nude queen have satyrs as bishops, each holding an open book, the knights are satyrs mounted upon goats, and the pawns are imps carrying stones, clubs or musical instruments.

SPAIN

Very early Spanish chesspieces of notable merit are known to have been made, but unfortunately they have not survived. Full-length figures of great beauty comprised the main pieces, which were often mounted upon wooden plinths. In the seventeenth century, Catalonian chesspieces made from bone or ivory to a basic design were produced for play in the Barcelona area of Spain [figure 66]. At first glance the set would appear to be a composite one incorporating pieces from Dutch, French, German and Turkish sets, but every piece is original, and moreover, there is ample evidence available to prove that the type has a very early origin. The set illustrated was made at the end of the eighteenth century, but the type was in general use a hundred years before then.

Spanish craftsmen working in the eighteenth century excelled in ecclesiastical work and the carving of groups, cups and tankards, but few applied their craft to the manufacture of chesspieces. Nevertheless, at least one school of carvers produced numbers of sets in the second half of the eighteenth century. These craftsmen carved chesspieces to a design completely different from anything produced elsewhere. The design and style is so distinctive that for years collectors have referred to these

60 *(opposite)* Extremely rare nineteenth-century Austro-Hungarian pieces made of uranium and gold-oxide glass.

61 *(right)* Sixteenth-century Danish pieces of walrus ivory, which can be seen in the National-museet, Copenhagen.

62 *(below)* Elaborate solid silver pieces encrusted with precious and semi-precious stones, complete with matching board; made in Austria in the twentieth century.

63 Gallery- or 'pulpit'-mounted pieces from an eighteenth century Spanish set carved from kiln-dried bone; there are no human figures and the pawns are single acanthus leaves.

64 Three pawns from an eighteenth-century Spanish hardwood set.

pieces as 'traditional Spanish' or 'pulpit pieces'. One such set is turned and carved from kiln-dried bone with the pieces of one side stained deep brown. Every piece belonging to this beautiful Spanish chess set is gallery- or 'pulpit'-mounted. Human symbols were not included in the design of this arboraceous set, and even the pawns are represented by single acanthus leaves [figure 63]. Nevertheless, it has much in common with the set shown in figure 65. The reason why Spanish craftsmen made chess sets to this very distinctive design is quite unknown, but the extra-ordinary similarity of workmanship found in all eighteenth-century Spanish chesspieces leaves little doubt that all were made by one small school of craftsmen. The eighteenth-century set shown in figure 65 is one of the finest of its kind extant. Turned and carved from kiln-dried bone in the last quarter of the century, every symbol, with the exception of the rooks, is mounted within an acanthus leaf gallery. The exceptional quality of this set is clearly evident in the shaped galleries, (a most unusual feature), the bridled horses' heads, and the quality of the pawns.

A combination of ivory and bone was sometimes used in the manufacture of this and similar sets. Bone, although difficult to carve, was always cheap, and, since it was hollow, it was ideally suited to the manufacture of gallery bodies. Ivory was always costly but relatively easy to carve; in consequence, one will often find the galleries, stems and bases made of bone, and the actual symbols (heads, etc.) carved from ivory. Rooks associated with the Spanish chesspieces described are castellated single or

65 Superb eighteenth-century Spanish pieces turned and carved from bone.

double towers surmounted by flags or tapering finials. In the second half of the eighteenth century, a few excellent hardwood sets were made [figure 64], very much like the bone sets of the same period.

Another type of late eighteenth-century chesspiece, usually turned and carved from ivory, has the major pieces mounted within acanthus leaf pulpits, but the pawns are simple elegant turned stems. Double-headed horses are often found as knights.

The magnificent twentieth-century Spanish chess set shown in figure 118 is made from copper and brass. It is reputed to have been produced as a special commission for a celebrated Portuguese figure in 1910. For many years Spanish metalworkers have produced fine and interesting sets from brass and copper, the most noteworthy being Morphy reproductions.

66 Spanish pieces made in the Barcelona area in the eighteenth century.

(preceding spread)
67 Russian chesspieces carved from mammoth ivory in the eighteenth century.

(following spread)
69 Persian Mohammedan pieces on a chessboard of the same period (eighteenth century).

ACCORDING TO LEGEND, carved chesspieces of considerable merit were made by Russian craftsmen during the Middle Ages, but as information concerning such sets is unsubstantiated, it is utterly impossible to assess. It is quite possible that a few important sets were made at that time but, in keeping with most other countries, the great majority of all decorative Russian chesspieces were produced after the beginning of the eighteenth century. It is interesting to note that eighteenth-century Russian craftsmen were unique in that they carved chess sets in which the pieces were exact representations of those used in the early Indian game, *chaturanga*. Figure 74 shows a well-carved Russian set made from walrus ivory in the last quarter of the eighteenth century. The pieces are: *tsar* (king), *ferz* (counsellor), *slon* (elephant), *kon* (horse), *ladia* (boat), and *pieshka* (foot-soldier). Both walrus and mammoth ivory were used for carving sets of this type and one side of each set is stained either deep brown or crimson.

Carved from mammoth ivory with the pieces of one side stained crimson, one particular Russian chess set of the eighteenth century is probably unique. The normal counsellor (or commander-in-chief) is replaced by a woman (queen), standing figures of bishops replace elephants, and finally, elephants replace the ships as rooks. The kings and queens sit upon thrones, the bishops are robed and mitred figures, the knights are fine, mounted warriors, and the rooks are elephants with jewelled eyes. The pawns are foot-soldiers of conventional early Russian type. As is usual in nearly all eighteenth-century Russian sets, the pieces of one side portray Russians while their opponents are Persians.

Russian metal chesspieces are difficult to find; important sets were made from gold and silver during the nineteenth century, and well-made bronze pieces were cast in the first quarter of that century. As will be seen from figure 70, which shows a rare Russian bronze set, the characteristics evident in earlier carved pieces are entirely absent, for nineteenth-century metal sets have nothing at all in common with the earlier carved sets. The *ferz* (counsellor) gave way to a normal queen – she had no place in early chess – with the rest of the set following conventional European lines.

Beautiful hardstone chesspieces were made by the celebrated Fabergé establishment and, needless to say, their quality was altogether above reproach. The complete set shown in figure 71 is a superb hardstone and silver masterpiece which carries the Master's mark. The pieces of one side are carved from tawny aventurine quartz, the opposing side from grey Kalgan jasper. Both sides are mounted in silver and set on circular silver feet. The chessboard is formed from nephrite squares, alternating with others of pale apricot serpentine, set in a silver frame

68 *(opposite)* Modern Israeli pieces made from woven silver wire; one side is gold-plated.

70 Part of a nineteenth-century Russian set cast in bronze; a type extremely rare.

moulded with acanthus and laurel leaf borders. A bun foot at each corner supports the board.

In the nineteen-twenties, porcelain chesspieces of the highest quality were made in the Old Imperial Porcelain Factory near Petrograd (now the Lomonosov works, Leningrad). These sets are possibly the most interesting of all modern ceramic pieces. They are generally referred to as 'propaganda' sets because the sides portrayed are Capitalists and Communists [figure 72]. The Capitalist king has a death's head, his queen is pouring gold from a cornucopia, the bishops are officers of the old régime, and the pawns are workers enchained. The predominant colour of the Capitalist side is black. The opposing Communist side has for its king a workman holding a sledge-hammer, his queen is a woman clutching a sheaf of corn, the bishops are Russian soldiers, and the pawns are happy women harvesters. The predominant colour is pink. The rooks of both sides are boats, the sails of the Capitalist boat are decorated with chains and an executioner's axe, those of their opponents with the hammer and sickle. At the beginning of production these sophisticated 'propaganda' chesspieces were of very high quality, well moulded, carefully painted and beautifully finished in burnished gilt, but later editions of the same set show a marked decline in general finish. Every piece of each set is marked with the hammer and sickle factory mark in red, and some sets carry figures to indicate the year of manufacture.

THE ARAB COUNTRIES

Chesspieces similar to those shown in figure 76 have been used throughout the Muslim World for centuries. Individual sets differ in size and quality, but all were made to strict geometric designs. The nineteenth-century pieces illustrated were made in or near Algiers from African ivory, but in North Africa similar

58

72 (left) Modern Russian 'propaganda' set made of porcelain; the opposing sides are Capitalists, whose pawns are workers in chains, and Communists, whose pawns are happy women harvesters.

73 (right) Early nineteenth-century Turkish pieces made from African ivory and designed to obey the Muslim Law, which forbids believers to handle graven images.

sets were made from wood, horn, hardstones, pottery and metal. Individual sets will differ slightly in shape, and certainly in quality, but on the whole all Mohammedan playing sets are very much alike. Chess did not become known to the Arabs until their conquest of Persia in the seventh century, and therefore any reference to the game in their Sacred Book is impossible. Since the *Koran* strictly forbade all true believers to handle figures in any shape or form, it is not surprising that when chess did become known, the legitimacy of the game among Arabs was suspect because of its image association, and it was only after many years of debate that a judicial decision was reached.

It was finally decreed that the game of chess was perfectly legitimate provided that the chesspieces used were of simple geometric shapes, and that the game was not played for the purpose of gambling.

Nomadic Arabs often carried a chess set for use when on the move; possibly the finest example of Moroccan portable chess known is the set shown in figure 77. It was made in the first quarter of the nineteenth century and, although used by the family of its original owners for several generations, remains in superb condition. The pieces are made from spun-silk gold and silver braid worked over wooden forms. Each piece is mounted

71 Fabergé hardstone and silver chesspieces, complete with matching board.

74 Knight, king and rook from an eighteenth-century Russian set in walrus ivory.

upon an old silver coin base. The velvet-covered, folding, wooden chessboard has green and red squares enclosed within a green border, embellished with a raised embroidery design in gold thread.

Yemeni craftsmen have made chesspieces from woven wire for centuries; most of the earliest sets were woven from copper or brass wire and these date back to the early part of the eighteenth century. The craft still flourishes in Israel, where modern versions of much earlier sets are made today [figure 68]. The example illustrated was made in 1959, and is a copy of much earlier Yemeni sets; it is somewhat heavier than later versions which are now made in quantities for the tourist trade. Smaller editions of this and similar modern sets are sometimes studded with semi-precious stones.

It has already been stated that under Muslim Law as written true believers are strictly forbidden to handle graven images. That chesspieces can be of simple form and yet pleasing to the eye is clearly shown in figure 73. These early nineteenth-century Turkish pieces are turned from African ivory with only a moderate amount of end carving. They have a delightful symmetry, they are well balanced and, although quite decorative, retain the essential features required to satisfy Muslim Law. Similar chesspieces to these were sometimes inlaid with silver wire or

75 Pieces from an eighteenth-century Persian silver set; the tops of one side and the bases of the other are gold-plated.

pigment. Early Turkish craftsmen made chessmen from ivory, brass, copper, wood and pottery. Usually the pieces produced were small and simple with very little decoration, as they were made solely for use, but from time to time handsome sets were made from silver wire interwoven to form intricate, though basically simple, shapes and designs. Copper and brass sets were either cast, or cut from the sheet, then hammered to shape and burnished. Often copper or brass sets chased to simple arabesque patterns were afterwards inlaid with metal or pigment. Few early pottery pieces have survived; they were fired at very low temperatures and were somewhat friable. At the time of manufacture this did not matter because replacement pieces were easily made.

PERSIA

Persian potters made chesspieces from a soft porcelain, but we cannot give them even an approximate date of origin. Soft porcelain was known to Persian potters in the seventeenth century, but it is doubtful if chess sets were made until very much later. The pieces were of simple form, fairly well potted, but brilliantly enamelled in lapis-lazuli blue, pale brownish-yellow, brown and metallic lustres. Mohammedan chesspieces of orthodox design were turned from African or Indian ivory and usually both sides were coloured [figure 69]. Persian metalworkers cast and chased quantities of simple playing sets; some very striking chesspieces were made from brass overlaid with fired enamels and these closely resemble early *cloisonné* work.

Figure 75 shows a most important early eighteenth-century Persian set made of silver. Every piece is finely chased, with the tops of one side and the bottoms of the other finished in gold.

76 Mohammedan pieces carved from African ivory in Algeria in the nineteenth century and turned to strict geometric shapes.

EASTERN CHESSPIECES

78 Very rare Burmese pieces carved from Indian ivory in the eighteenth century.

77 *(opposite)* A portable set made in Morocco; the pieces are woven with gold and silver thread over wooden bases; the board is covered in velvet.

BURMA

As ALREADY MENTIONED, a modified form of *shatranj,* or the medieval game of India called *chit-tha-reen,* was played in Burma from the beginning of the seventh century. Thirty-two chesspieces were used upon a board subdivided into sixty-four squares. The four centre squares of the board were linked (crossed) together. Originally, the chesspieces were suitably marked cubes or discs, but there is ample evidence to suggest that shaped and carved figures were used at a very early date.

At the beginning of a game, each player was allowed to arrange his major pieces in positions most suited to his method of play and prowess. He could disport his pieces to strengthen either flank, or, if he felt so disposed, protect or expose his king. Several preliminary moves were made before the game started, but after a brief skirmish the real battle began.

Figure 79 shows the Burmese chessboard and chesspieces at this stage of the game. The names of the pieces, together with their moves, are as follows:

1 MENG (king) moves one step in all directions but cannot castle.
2 CHEKOY (general) moves diagonally one step at a time, forward or backward.
3 RATHA (war chariot) moves in a direct line, forward, backward, or to either side.
4 CHEIN (elephant) moves one square forward, and two diagonally either way, but captures only on the diagonal. The forward step allows him to control both black and white diagonals.
5 MHEE (horse). His move is the same as the knight in the medieval game.
6 YEIN (foot-soldier) moves one step directly forward, but captures diagonally to either side. Only the *yein* on the right hand side of the chessboard qualifies for promotion to the rank of *chekoy* (in the event of the *chekoy* being already captured), but for this promotion the *yein* need not advance to the last rank.

Early craftsmen working in India and China produced chesspieces in extremely large quantities with the sole object of satis-

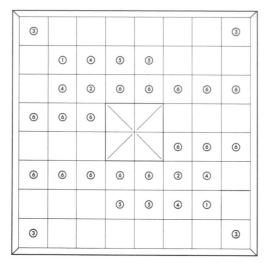

80, 81 Pieces from two different hardwood sets made in Burma in the eighteenth century; before these dates, Burmese sets were invariably carved from softwoods.

fying an overseas demand, but a completely different set of circumstances existed in Burma. Carved chesspieces were made simply for use; their manufacture was not organized on a commercial basis, and the few sets which found their way out of Burma were taken by visitors who regarded the acquisition of a chess set as something of a novelty, or as a souvenir to commemorate a visit. Burmese chesspieces made before the eighteenth century were invariably carved from softwoods, while eighteenth-century Burmese chesspieces of a similar type were carved from hardwoods [figure 80 and 81]. One side of each wooden set was stained brown or green, while the opposing side was normally black.

Very few ivory chesspieces were made in Burma before the eighteenth century, but from the beginning of that century very fine sets were carved from Indian ivory [figure 78]. The bishops in the set shown are symbolized by horse-drawn Juggernaut carts. This is a most unusual feature, and is seldom found in early Burmese chess sets. Usually the bishop is symbolized by a temple [figure 83] or horseless Juggernaut cart. Juggernaut, the idol of Krishna, was dragged yearly in procession on a cart under the wheels of which devotees are said to have thrown themselves. These carts are frequently found in Indian sets, but rarely in Burmese.

A most unusual hardstone chess set is shown in figure 85. It was ground from brown and smoky agate in Burma during the

82 Early nineteenth-century pieces carved from Indian ivory and ebony in Ceylon.

last quarter of the nineteenth century. In form it resembles many ivory sets carved in India at about the same time; the bishops are portrayed as camels, a most unusual feature in Burmese sets, and the pawns are of a shape common to European sets.

It is virtually impossible to ascertain where any particular early Burmese chess set was made, but it is fairly safe to assume that the majority were made in and around Pagan. By the first quarter of the nineteenth century, chesspieces were carved from Indian ivory on a commercial basis in many parts of Burma. In these sets, the style of carving, the meticulous attention to detail, together with the overall finish clearly indicate that the carvers were of Chinese origin but moved to Burma and settled there [figure 86]. Each set has the same characteristics, but there is a wide and remarkable variation in size and quality. Although the finest equal the best Chinese sets, the small unimportant sets, though made to the same basic design, are unworthy of attention as they are poorly carved from inferior material. The best are carved and pierced in highly complex and ingenious patterns; birds, flowers and scenes from Chinese legends appear on the stems of the larger pieces. Inferior versions of otherwise identical sets are merely surface engraved. Although for many years chesspieces such as these have been referred to as 'traditional Burmese' in fact the whole concept is quite alien to Burma.

83 Indian ivory pieces carved in Burma early in the eighteenth century; here the bishop is symbolized by the temple usually found in Burmese sets.

84 Diagram of the Chinese game (choke-choo-hong-ki), showing the pieces arranged for the beginning of the game. (See text for key.)

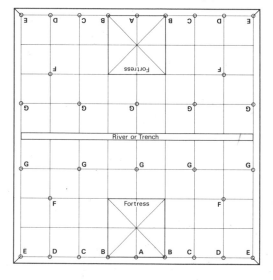

85 (below left and right) Burmese pieces carved from brown and smoky agate towards the end of the nineteenth century; the bishops are camels, which is most unusual in Burmese sets.

CHINA

Although the Chinese claim to have invented chess some 2072 years ago during the Hansing campaign, *choke-choo-hong-ki* (the name applied to the Chinese game) is merely a variation of *shat-ranj*, the medieval game of India. Thirty-two suitably engraved wood or ivory discs were used upon a board subdivided into sixty-four squares. The board was divided into two halves by a river or trench, called *hoa-ki*, and the two centre squares of the rear rank were linked together and to the two squares immediately in front of them in the second rank to form a fortress in which the king and his two counsellors moved. The chesspieces were positioned on the dividing lines and did not occupy the squares [figure 84].

The names of the pieces and their moves are as follows:

A   CHONG (king or general). He stands at the centre of the rear rank, and moves one step in all directions, but is confined to the limits of this fortress.

B   SOU (prince or counsellor). There are two of them. A *sou* stands beside the *chong* and has similar moves and limits.

C   TCHONG (mandarin or elephant). They are two in number. A *tchong* stands next to each *sou*. He moves two steps at a time, forward or backward, but cannot advance across the river.

D   MAI (horse). They are two in number. A *mai* stands next to each *tchong*. He has precisely the same moves as a knight in medieval chess, but cannot cross the river.

E   TCHE (chariot). They are two in number. A *tche* stands next to each *mai* at the outer edge of the board. He has exactly the same moves as the rook in medieval chess, and can cross the river.

F   PAO (rocket boy or mortar). They are two in number. A *pao* stands in front of each *mai* on the next line but one. A *pao* moves across the entire board; forward, backwards, and to either side. If an opponent's piece intervenes in a direct line, a *pao* captures the piece immediately behind it.

G   PING (pawn or foot-soldier). They are five in number, and stand on lines of the third rank as indicated. They move one step at a time forward, but capture sideways; they may cross the river, but there is no promotion on reaching the final rank.

The game ends when a player's pieces are totally destroyed,

86 Indian ivory pieces carved in Burma for export in the nineteenth century; the style indicates that carvers were of Chinese origin

87 Indian ivory pieces of the type made in China during the first half of the nineteenth century for export to the western world; later in the century the quality of such sets declined, but in the earlier sets the ball mounts are very finely carved.

when his *chong* is mated or the game reaches a position of stalemate. Perpetual check did not enter into the game; the move was varied.

Figure 119 shows an example of a seventeenth-century Chinese chess set *(choke-choo-hong-ki)*, seen here without the board. Turned from Indian ivory, the pieces are engraved with characters in a simple, elegant hand. The characters of one side are coloured red, those of the other, deep blue. From the latter part of the eighteenth century until well into the nineteenth, countless carved ivory chess sets were produced in China exclusively for the Western market. Thousands of sets were carved from Indian ivory by craftsmen working in and around Canton, in French Indo-China, and in Macao. Apart from sets made in the Portuguese colony, of Macao, all were similar in design, but differed in size and quality. All nineteenth-century carved Chinese sets look very much alike, but quality varies to a marked degree, large important sets reaching near perfection, while small unimportant sets are badly carved from poor quality ivory taken from the open end of the tusk. All Chinese chess sets destined for the European market had much in common, but as different mounts were used, they can be classified into at least four types. Several versions of each type were made.

One type can be considered superior to all others; it was boldly carved, well proportioned, and perfectly finished. Each of the thirty-two pieces comprising the set was mounted upon a heavy octagonal base, with the figure and base carved from a single piece throughout. Each face of the base was deeply carved to show birds, flowers, beasts or incidents from Chinese legends. Apart from perfection of workmanship and finish, Chinese chesspieces of this type were far more robust than their ball- or rosette-mounted counterparts.

The most common of all Chinese nineteenth-century pieces is the Cantonese ball-mounted set. Each figure is mounted atop a carved and pierced concentric ball rising from a carved circular base. The largest and most important set of this type was said to have been carved for the Emperor Tao Kwang in the nineteenth century. The kings of this set stand $12\frac{1}{2}$ inches high; the

88 Rare nineteenth-century Chinese pieces carved from red coral; the other side is of white coral.

89 Very fine Cantonese ball-mounted set carved from Indian ivory of an exceptionally high quality; this set is now in the Chess Room of the British House of Commons.

kings and queens are mounted upon balls containing seven other balls; the bishops, knights and rooks stand on balls containing six others, and the pawn's mounts have five inner balls.

Figure 87 shows Chinese chesspieces of the type which was carved from Indian ivory in Canton early in the nineteenth century. The early versions of this type made not later than 1850 are always of fine quality but sets made towards the close of the century, and after a market had been established, show a marked decline in finish. Ball mounts associated with large sets are sometimes quite exceptional; every part of the outer surface is minutely carved to portray birds, beasts, flowers or insects. Each large ball contains as many as seven other gradually diminishing balls, all carved and pierced. Cantonese concentric balls have been carved from Indian ivory for centuries. Although the manufacturing process is slow and tedious, it is not a particularly difficult understaking for a skilled craftsman. A solid piece of ivory is turned to the desired size on a lathe, the resulting ball is pierced to its centre at equally divided points with a taper drill to give the worker spaces through which he frees the innermost ball. He then proceeds to the next ball, and continues the process until all the balls are free. Specially shaped tools are used for this work.

Three main themes were portrayed in Chinese chesspieces made for the Western market: Chinese against Mongolians; Chinese against forces headed by an English king; Chinese against forces headed by Napoleon. Apart from the kings and queens, opposing forces are more or less the same for each side. Sets intended for England portrayed an English king and queen on the white side; those intended for France featured Napoleon and Josephine. Perhaps the finest and most important ball-mounted Cantonese set of this type is shown in figure 89. It occupies an honoured position in the Chess Room of the British House of Commons, and is one of the largest and most imposing sets of its kind. Both sides are carved from Indian ivory with the pieces of one side stained crimson.

Slightly less spectacular, but often much more compact, some Chinese sets had each figure mounted upon a carved rosette mount. Apart from giving stability to the pieces, such mounts increased their height and transformed small unimportant pieces into worthwhile sets. Another type made use of plain flat bases

90 Pieces from a nineteenth-century set made by Chinese craftsmen in Macao for the western market. Most of such sets were exported to England and the flag surmounting the white rooks is almost always the Union Jack.

91 Pieces from one of the rare 'rat' sets made in China in the eighteenth century.

which were carved as an integral part of the figures. Very fine sets of this type were made in French Indo-China; they always portray a European king and queen in the white side. The pieces are somewhat stunted but, although less elaborate than Cantonese pieces, are much finer. The warrior knights sit astride handsome horses rampant, and the pawns of one side are armed with muskets.

Perhaps the most rare, and certainly the most unorthodox of all Chinese chesspieces are those made towards the close of the eighteenth century in the form of rats. Several very fine examples are known to exist, but they were not produced on a commercial scale and, in fact, all such sets were probably made by one brilliant craftsman. The rats are seen in different postures, and there is plenty of action [figure 91]. The ruby and amber eye insertions give the rats an extraordinarily lifelike appearance and the sets are superbly carved from Indian ivory with the decorative etching of one side stained light brown.

Coral, which can be red, pink or white, can also be rough and porous or compact and smooth. Smooth coral has always been prized as a material for carving exquisite trinkets and figures, but it is difficult to work and polish. Rarely does one find a complete chess set carved from this beautiful substance, but figure 88 shows part of an early nineteenth-century set, exquisitely carved from red and white coral.

Early in the nineteenth century, some very pretty little wooden chess sets were carved in Singapore and the Straits' Settlements. Each set was carefully painted and nicely finished but they have little importance apart from being carved from wood.

In spite of the fact that Portuguese traders established themselves in China during the sixteenth century, it was not until very late in the eighteenth that the manufacture of chesspieces became part of their stock-in-trade. Vast quantities of distinctive chess sets were made in the early nineteenth century by Chinese craftsmen working in and around the Portuguese settlement of Macao. It is quite possible that at the outset Portuguese settlers may have originated the type for their own use, but it is much more likely that Chinese craftsmen were able to visualize the commercial possibilities of a set which was both distinctive and economical to make. Figure 90 shows typical Macao pieces;

92 *(below)* Very fine Bengal pieces carved from Indian ivory at the end of the eighteenth century; Bengal pieces are smaller and less ornate than Delhi pieces.

symbols of human heads or busts surmount Burmese-type pieces made for export; the white side pieces are always portrayed as Europeans, and the kings and queens, which are generally believed to represent Portuguese royalty, are, in fact, English. The error is occasioned by the fact that the white pawns wear helmets similar to those worn by sixteenth-century Portuguese infantry. Almost always a Union Jack is engraved on the flags surmounting the white rooks. As far as can be ascertained, chess-

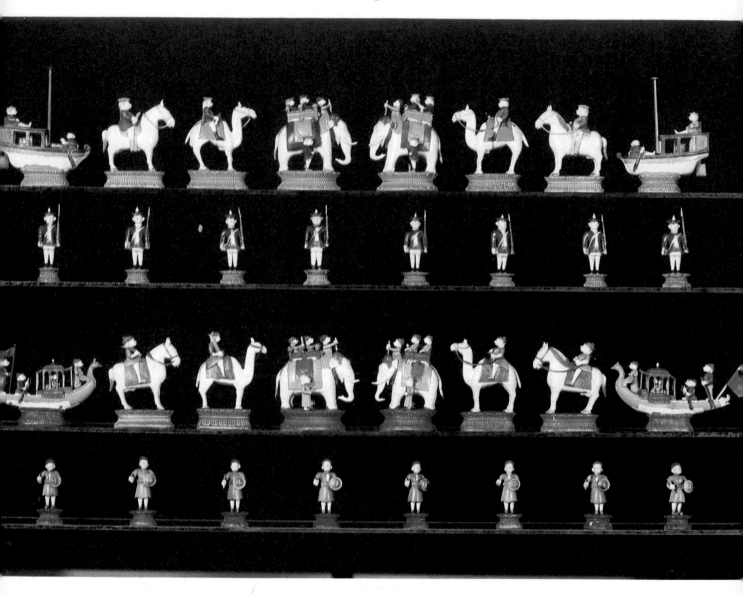

93 *(opposite)* Bronze set wrought in Madras early in the eighteenth century; unlike later ivory sets, the pieces here all represent Indian forces, with no Europeans.

pieces of this type are not found in Portugal; the majority of all sets made in Macao and the surrounding districts were exported to England. The bases and stems of the pieces are no different from those carved on a commercial basis in Burma, and in fact the bases, stems and rooks of Burmese commercial sets are identical to those made in Macao and French Indo-China.

98 This chariot is the traditional symbol for the John side bishops in Delhi sets; the bishops of the native side are Juggernaut carts.

98 This chariot is the traditional symbol for the John side bishops in Delhi sets; the bishops of the native side are Juggernaut carts.

94, 95, 96, 97 *(opposite)* Several different basic types of chesspieces were made in Delhi for export in the first half of the nineteenth century. The type illustrated in the top photograph has one side of ivory and one of sandalwood or horn; the middle two have both sides turned from ivory, but one is stained. The finest and most elaborate sets were made in Kashmir, as can be seen in the delicate carving of the pieces in the bottom illustration.

INDIA

No chess sets, complete or incomplete, used in the early Indian game (*chaturanga*) have survived, but it is safe to assume that, mainly, suitably marked flat or convex discs were used. With few exceptions, all decorative Indian chess sets which come within the reach of the collector were produced during a period of one hundred and eighty years; that is, from the last quarter of the eighteenth century until midway through the nineteenth. This does not mean that no decorative sets were made before the eighteenth century. There is evidence available to prove that an Indian carved ivory chess set was given to Louis XIV by the Siamese ambassador in 1686.

Chesspieces made throughout the period with which we are mostly concerned differ considerably in design and quality. They range from exquisitely carved, highly ornate sets by such master craftsmen as Yakymour to crudely executed pieces made by relatively unskilled native carvers. Ivory, which for generations has been highly prized in the East, was used in the production of chesspieces which rank among the most spectacular ever made. By far the most popular theme used was the struggle between the old East India Company and native rulers. The East India Company, which was incorporated by Elizabeth in 1600, was able to obtain a footing in India in 1613, and secured a charter of privileges from the Great Mogul. The Company suffered severe losses during the reign of Charles I, and was forced to open a subscription for new stock. The Company's charter was annulled during the Commonwealth, but was renewed some three years later with a new stock of some £370,000. Thenceforth the fortunes of the company improved, and after 1662, when Bombay came under its influence, considerable strides were made. Bombay became a most important trading post, and all went well until France sought to gain power in India. A fierce struggle for supremacy ensued, but the achievements of Clive gained victory for England, and after 1765 the company became possessed of Bengal, Behar and Orissa, in addition to Madras (which it already possessed). Thenceforth British power was undisputed except by native princes. Before the Indian Mutiny of 1857, the 'John Company' was a familiar name for the East India Company.

It is this long struggle between the Company and the native rulers which is so often portrayed in fine Indian chess sets. Figure 99 shows a fine example which was carved in Delhi towards the close of the eighteenth century. All 'John' chess sets use the same theme, but many variations in interpretation are found; the main differences will be found in bishops and rooks. Bishops are usually portrayed as soldiers astride camels, but sometimes they represent chariots, or Juggernaut carts, sometimes tigers or oxen, and sometimes rhinoceros. Rooks are usually

75

99 *(above)* A fine Delhi 'John' set, carved from Indian ivory with both sides polychromed in the late eighteenth century.

100 *(opposite)* A Madras set carved from Indian ivory, well painted and lavishly gilt; Madras pieces are crudely carved from small sections of ivory cemented together and the figures within the howdahs, the pawns' heads and weapons are all separate pieces.

101 Delhi 'bust' type set featuring Sir Colin Campbell and Nana Sahib as opposing kings.

102 This finely carved boat is a typical rook from a Delhi set of the 'John' type.

103 One each of the opposing pawns from the John and native sides of a fine Delhi set carved in the eighteenth century.

round towers surmounted by a soldier holding a flag, or by boats.

Pieces from another Delhi set carved from Indian ivory at about the same date represent what is generally termed 'a traditional Delhi chess set of the John type': elephants (king and counsellor), chariots (John side bishops), Juggernaut carts (native side bishops), knights mounted upon horses (John side), knights mounted upon camels (native side), boats (rooks – both sides) and foot-soldiers [figures 98, 102, 103]. Delhi chesspieces such as these are always faultlessly carved and finished. The bases of one side are always dyed red, green, black or brown, while the figures are left natural.

These beautiful chesspieces were made expressly as commemorative or presentation sets. They are far too bizarre for actual use; if positioned upon a chessboard the major pieces would sometimes require a square larger than four by four inches. The pawns would look ridiculous and would be completely overshadowed by the larger pieces.

Perhaps the most spectacular, and certainly the most quaint, of all Indian chesspieces are those made at the close of the eighteenth century in and around Madras. Figure 100 shows a fine Madras set carved from Indian ivory which is well painted and lavishly gilt. Madras chesspieces are not carved from the solid; they are crudely carved from small sections of ivory which are cemented together. It is not unusual to find small sections of hardwood mixed with the ivory pieces. The small figures within the howdahs, canopies, animals' tails, pawns' heads and weapons are all separate pieces. Each of these sets features the struggle between the East India Company and native rulers. When both sides of the same set are painted, the predominant colours are red and green with black lining covered by superimposed white dots. When only one side of a particular set is painted, the painted side will be red or green, and the uncoloured side will be coated in clear lacquer with superimposed gold dots and red lining. Amusing features of Madras chesspieces are the appendages: cannon and ladders carried by the elephants, musical instruments, including drums, and the odd assortment of weapons carried by every piece. Madras chesspieces make a big appeal to collectors, who regard them as possibly the most desirable of all Indian pieces.

104 Nepalese pieces rather similar to their Delhi counterparts, but less ornate; the *wazir* is portrayed as a mounted warrior.

(following spread)
105 Very rare Mongolian pieces carved from wood at the beginning of the twentieth century.

Countless numbers of chess sets were made in India by a process of turning and carving; pieces were turned to shape on the lathe, then finished by carvers. Many sets appear to have been carved but were made throughout on the lathe. Several basic types of Indian chesspieces were made in vast quantities for export in and around Delhi during the first half of the nineteenth century [figures 94–97]. Several sizes of each type were made and the quality of material and workmanship is directly proportional to size. Large sets with 5-inch kings are finely turned from good quality ivory, while smaller sizes are not so well made, and the material is of poor quality. In some sets the pieces of one side are always of ivory; the opposing side is turned from sandalwood or horn [figure 94]. Both sides of the sets seen in figures 95 and 96 are turned from ivory with the pieces of one side stained red, green, black or brown.

The most elaborate, and certainly the most exquisite, turned and carved chesspieces ever made were produced towards the close of the eighteenth century in Kashmir. The carving of the major pieces resembles lace. The pawns represent foot-soldiers of the East India Company and native troops [figure 97]. Apart from the pawns, both sides of Kashmir sets are identical, but the bases of one side are stained green, red or deep brown. Good quality Kashmir sets with their 6½-inch kings are among the finest of all Indian chesspieces.

Chesspieces from Bengal resemble in some respects Delhi 'John' sets, but they are smaller, and somewhat less ornate. They are always meticulously carved from Indian ivory and sparsely painted in greens and pinks. The rooks are always portrayed as boats which contain archer-guards, and the two sides feature the East India Company and native forces. The green and pink colouring is most carefully applied.

The finest quality Indian chess sets do not always incorporate human figures, and figure 107 shows a beautifully carved Kashmir set which differs from most others. No figures of any kind are featured. The extremely ornate pawns compare quite favourably with the foot-soldiers of figure 97.

Other early eighteenth-century chesspieces portray human beings, but no Europeans feature in any of the sets, and the rook is represented by a boat. Carved from solid pieces of ivory in and

79

around Delhi, they perhaps inspired the much more sophisticated 'John' sets made towards the close of the century.

A set which was carved in Nepal from Indian ivory in the last quarter of the eighteenth century, and is shown in figure 104, differs in many important respects from its Delhi counterpart. The general quality and craftsmanship equals that of the Delhi set, but the whole set is less ornate, and there is a better relationship between the sizes of the individual pieces. Even the pawns compare in size quite favourably with larger pieces. In this, and similar sets, the *wazir* is portrayed as a mounted warrior. Smaller and less important 'bust' type chesspieces were carved in Nepal in the first quarter of the nineteenth century, and the pieces of one side are usually carved from horn.

In the last quarter of the nineteenth century, some fairly well carved 'bust' type sets were made in and around Delhi. One important set of this type features Sir Colin Campbell and Nana Sahib as opposing kings and was inspired by the Indian Mutiny of 1857 [figure 101]. As is usual in Indian 'bust' sets, bases of one side are stained black, but the actual symbols are left in highly polished natural ivory.

Brass and bronze chesspieces were wrought and cast very early in the eighteenth century in the Madras area of India. In one interesting bronze chess set, wrought in Madras not later than the beginning of the eighteenth century, the pieces at first sight remotely resemble late eighteenth-century Madras ivory sets, but there is a very real difference. No Europeans whatsoever are portrayed; the two sides comprising the complete set both represent Indian forces. Without the slightest doubt, the set was made simply for use, as the workmanship throughout is crude and the finish is rough, but for purposes of play it would be quite effective – the individual pieces are easy to distinguish,

106 Fine nineteenth-century Jaipur pieces made of gold, enamelled and encrusted with jewels.

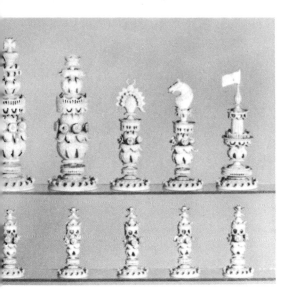

107 This fine Kashmir set differs from most Indian sets in having no human figures at all.

and, being heavy, the whole set would prove very stable.

Figure 93 shows an example of a set cast by the 'lost wax' (*cire-perdue*) process which is unique. The 'lost wax' is a very old process, simple but wasteful. At the outset, a wax model is made to the desired shape or form and from this model a one-piece mould is made. A hole is left in the mould so that after it is made and dried, the wax model may be melted and poured out. Molten brass or whatever metal is being used is then poured into the mould and left to cool. After cooling, there is only one way to recover the casting, and that is to break the mould. Needless to say, as a mould is broken each time a figure is cast, and as the wax model is melted when the mould is made, only one figure or casting can be made from each wax model. The process derives its name from the fact that the wax model is indeed 'lost'. Such brass pieces were roughly cast, but scraped to remove all the roughage and to give excellent detail.

Both sides of this set are enamelled in brilliant colours, one predominantly blue, the other red. All faces, hands and appendages are picked out in realistic tones, and where necessary the brass is burnished. It is not unique, but certainly one of the earliest metal chess sets of Madras origin to feature the East India Company and native forces.

India did not excel in the production of hardstone chesspieces; a number were made early in the nineteenth century, but they were of simple form, and poorly finished.

Small jewel-studded sets were, however, made from gold and silver in the nineteenth century. One superlative Indian chess set is made of Jaipur gold, exquisitely enamelled and studded with jewels [figure 106]. The goldsmith's skill is evident throughout this delightful set. Each piece has a fitted hardstone plaque inserted beneath its base and these plaques are highly polished, making for easy movement during play and obviating the need for base coverings.

Excellent twentieth-century chesspieces are being made in India and these, apart from inferior copies of earlier Delhi sets,

108 Japanese *shogi* pieces made from Indian ivory in the eighteenth century.

are for the most part 'bust' sets. The extravagant mythology of India is portrayed in a variety of styles; the sets are well carved and highly finished, but are made on a commercial scale, with little attention to detail.

JAPAN

Shogi, or Japanese chess, which is a variation of *shatranj*, has been played in Japan more or less unchanged for seven hundred years. It passed to Japan, probably by way of Korea, some time in the thirteenth century, and still retains immense popularity. During the last twenty-five years *shogi* has become quite popular in the United States of America, and is making progress in Europe. *Shogi* chesspieces are flat tablets of an elongated penta-

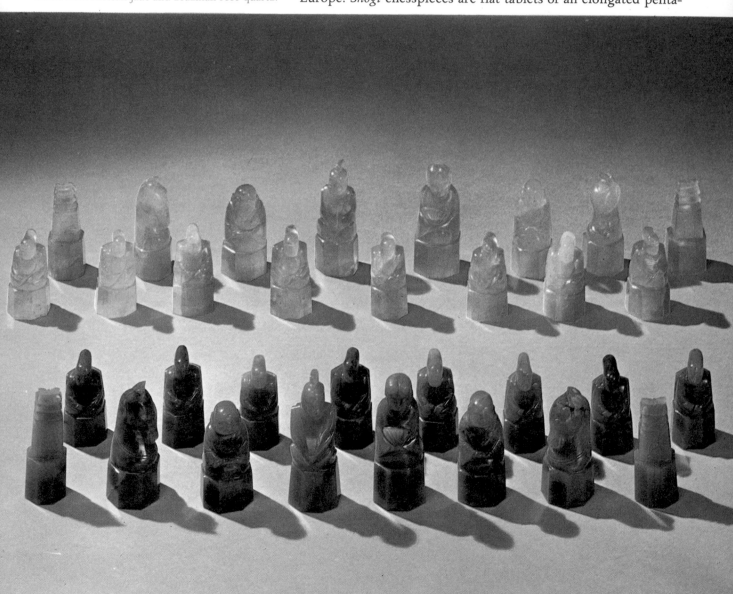

109 Modern Japanese hardstone chesspieces made from African jade and Brazilian rose quartz.

110 Rare Mongolian wooden pieces, carved in about 1750.

gon shape tapering from base to apex. They are identified by characters engraved on their obverse faces, while pieces capable of promotion have their reverse faces engraved to show promotion values. Upon promotion, the piece is turned over to reveal its changed value. During play the pieces lie flat upon the board with their apexes pointing towards their adversaries. *Shogi* chesspieces are always of the same shape, but they differ to a considerable extent in quality, and range from simple wooden sets roughly made and engraved, to well-made, highly polished and beautifully engraved tablets [figure 108].

Modern Japanese craftsmen are fully alive to the demand for beautiful chesspieces, and since the end of the Second World War have produced very attractive hardstone sets, using contrasting stones imported from all over the world including jade, tiger eye, and various kinds of quartz. Figure 109 shows a set made from African jade and Brazilian rose quartz. The finish of each set equals that of the best early jade sets.

Apart from modern hardstone sets, Japan is now producing well-carved ivory sets in a number of sizes; the smallest are about three inches in height, the largest have kings which sometimes exceed seven inches. Although these sets are well made, beautifully finished, and carefully turned out in fitted box/boards with padded carrying cases, they have little aesthetic appeal.

OTHER EASTERN COUNTRIES

Conventional wooden playing chesspieces were made in Java from a very early date. Javanese chess is of Indian origin. It is called *chatur*, and the pieces are named: *ratu* (king), *pateh* (minister – queen), two *prahu* (rooks), two *mantri* (bishops), two *jaran* (knights), and eight *bidak* (pawns). The sixteen pieces constitute one side of the game, which is played upon a normal chessboard with sixty-four squares, but in the original game, the king (*ratu*) was always positioned on the left-hand side of the queen (*pateh*), and in consequence faced the opposing queen. The moves were similar to those in the modern game, except that on his first move, and if he had not been checked, the king could move two squares; if a pawn reached his opponent's first rank, it had to retreat three squares diagonally before it became a queen, unless it reached the opposing rook's square, in which case it became a queen at once. Castling was allowed, provided the king had not been checked, but was performed in two stages – a castle was first brought up to the king, and at a future move the king passed over the rook. A piece or a pawn had to remain on the board until the game ended; if a king was left alone, the game was considered stalemate, and the opponent had won, provided some of his pieces remained.

About the middle of the nineteenth century very striking chesspieces were made from carved and painted bamboo. The kings, queens, bishops and pawns were all distorted representations of human beings with long, protruding snouts and receding chins. Kings and bishops each had two pairs of eyes, one pair facing forwards, the other pair backwards. The knights were horses' heads on human trunks, and the rooks were elephant heads with similar bodies. Kings, queens, bishops and pawns were all full-length figures. Knights and rooks terminated halfway down the trunk: the two legs of each figure were in one plane, there being no left or right foot. These interesting bamboo pieces are well carved, and brightly painted in pinks, whites, pale yellows and reds – all with silver trim.

Very little is known about early Ceylonese chess, but the medieval game (*shatranj*) was certainly played there for many centuries. It is doubtful if any finely carved chesspieces were made before the nineteenth century in Ceylon and very few were ever made. One most rare and interesting set, which was carved in Ceylon, probably in Colombo or thereabouts, early in the nineteenth century, is perfectly carved from Indian ivory and ebony. Both sides are identical. The kings are portrayed as Buddha (representing the highest mystic state of human existence), while the queens are represented by disciples in the state of *nirvana*, the condition of supreme attainment in which all forms of desire, ambition and unrest are extinguished [figure 82].

In Cambodia chess has been played for at least five centuries with simple well-made pieces. Cambodian chesspieces all follow the same basic design: they are small, compact and entirely functional, with kings, queens, bishops and rooks all simple pieces turned to a pearlike shape. Knights are finely carved horses' heads (always with their lower jaw resting upon their necks), and the pawns are either small convex discs or flat shells. Usually, but not always, the symbols turned to represent queens are smaller than the other major pieces, a most unusual feature found only in Cambodian and early Siamese sets.

A considerable difference of opinion exists about the origin of many early chesspieces attributed to Siam. Antiquarians of Thailand generally agree that the only type of chess set which they can authenticate as being made and used throughout Siam for the last six centuries closely resembles that used in Cambodia – small shell-like turned pieces with the knight the only figurative piece. Nevertheless, in the Thai National Museum in Bangkok there is a carved chess set which closely resembles the Burmese set shown in figure 83, but this may have been carved by a Burmese craftsman working in Siam. All carved wood, carved ivory and cast-metal chess sets usually attributed to Siam have, with very few exceptions, a Burmese origin. It is just possible that a Burmese craftsman could have made a set in Siam, but this is somewhat improbable in the case of early sets.

Complete and authentic Mongolian chess sets are most rare, but during his Eastern travels Mr Schuyler Van Rensselaer Camman of the United States of America was fortunate enough to locate and secure two complete sets some twenty-five years ago. One set is a wonderful carved wooden set made in Outer Mongolia about the middle of the eighteenth century. The extraordinary detail in every piece, together with the wonderful colouring which is so painstakingly applied, puts this superb set in a class by itself, and certainly among the most important of all Eastern chess sets [figure 110]. The second set [figure 105] has a much later origin. It was made at the beginning of the present century in Inner Mongolia. As will be seen, it has much in common with the earlier set, but lacks the wonderful detail, and has slightly less colour appeal. No other complete Mongolian chess sets are known or recorded and never before have similar examples been illustrated.

MODERN CHESSPIECES

Easy and rapid travel, a constantly increasing tourist movement, and a rapidly increasing field of collectors have done much to encourage craftsmen to make good chesspieces in post-war years. Not every collector can afford to pay the very high prices commanded by fine antique sets, and many new collectors seek high-grade modern products. As is always the case, if there is a demand for craftsmanship, craftsmen satisfy that demand, and a large number of decorative chess sets have been produced in several countries since the last war. Some of these sets are excellent, many downright bad, but all in all, the average quality is directly proportional to what the purchaser is prepared to pay.

About twenty different types of ivory chessmen are made in Hong Kong; these vary in size and quality from cheap little sets hacked from inferior material to finely carved and well finished pieces with 7-inch kings. One side of each set is stained light or deep brown. Modern Japanese ivory sets have much in common with those made in Hong Kong; the quality is about the same, but small Japanese sets equal in workmanship the largest sets. Modern Japanese hardstone chesspieces leave little to be desired [figure 109].

Current Indian productions have already been referred to; the very best are good but many sets of cheaper quality are quite simply bad. In the Philippines a fair-sized local industry is being created for the manufacture of wooden chess sets, and well-carved, carefully finished hardwood sets are being made by craftsmen there [figure 111]. It is not absolutely certain when chess first became known in the Philippines, but it is reasonable to assume that it arrived from Borneo about four centuries ago.

A wide variety of modern chesspieces has been made during the last few years in the Middle East and in the continent of Africa. At least one Egyptian carver of considerable merit made good ivory chess sets to special order a few years ago. Large, boldly carved pieces were made from good quality African ivory; they show plenty of imagination in design and are reminiscent of ancient Egypt. Several types of metal chesspieces are made in North Africa, but these for the most part are unworthy of attention. The finest of all wooden African sets were carved from thornwood in Lagos about fifteen years ago. They are beautiful little 'bust' type sets, carved in the most graceful lines and most carefully coloured in natural tints. Carved ebony and thornwood chess sets are now made in great quantities in Tanzania. They are well-made little sets but, apart from size, every set is exactly alike.

To satisfy the demands of Belgian settlers, ivory carvers working in the Congo have for a great number of years made simple, distinctive chessmen. They are always very similar in shape, well-carved and highly polished. These 'bust' type Congolese sets were never made for export, but over the last few years a good few have been brought out of the Congo.

Some crudely cast, but very amusing little bronze chess sets are made in the Upper Volta region of Africa. The pieces are crude by most normal standards and no attempt is made to remove the roughage, but the bright paint with which they are decorated makes a valiant effort to cover inherent faults. As chess sets they cannot perhaps be taken seriously, but they serve to illustrate the imagination of a primitive people.

112 Wooden pieces carved in Haiti in the first half of the nineteenth century; their design is probably based on a European set made much earlier.

In the West Indies chesspieces have been made since the beginning of the nineteenth century. For the most part they are carved from wood and were copied from earlier French and German sets. A very unusual set of chesspieces was carved in Haiti from wood in the first half of the nineteenth century. The craftsmanship is crude but effective and it is probable that the pieces were based on, or copied from a much earlier Continental set [figure 112].

Very few fine old South American chesspieces were ever made, but modern sets have been made during the twentieth century, and over the last few years Mexico has created a small industry for the manufacture of onyx pieces. The onyx from which these sets are made is dyed to most unusual colours – blue, brown, green, red and coral pink. In relation to their cost, these modern onyx sets represent excellent value, and one representative set is a worthy addition to any collection. The set shown in figure 114 is a most interesting example which was made from silver in Ecuador early in the twentieth century. The type may well, in years to come, be regarded as traditional.

In post-war years most European countries have produced decorative chess sets, many of which have been discussed in earlier chapters. The best have been made in Germany by craftsmen working in Hamburg. Fine carved ivory sets have been produced to a variety of designs; they equal in quality, though not in size, some of the finest early German sets.

113 Early nineteenth-century pieces carved from Indian ivory in French Indo-China.

Poland has, for a number of years, made attractive little painted wooden chess sets. They have little real merit but, like their Spanish counterparts, are cheap to buy and highly decorative. Denmark, Austria, Hungary and Switzerland all make inferior versions of their early sets; they are carved from softwoods and appear to be made down to a price rather than up to a standard, but a few of the better examples are worthy of a modern collection. Fine quality painted wooden sets are made

111 *(opposite)* Contemporary wooden pieces made in the Philippines.

114 *(above and below)* Pieces from a silver set made in Ecuador early in the twentieth century; it is only in this century that fine chess sets have been produced in South America.

115 Swiss bird and animal chesspieces carved from pearwood; few modern sets are made from hardwoods.

in Italy and the best almost equal in quality older wooden pieces; but whereas the finest old wooden sets were made from hardwoods which today are scarce and costly, modern pieces are carved from softwoods. They lack the charm of earlier sets; they are a little too frivolous, and have a factory-made appearance.

Marble (and synthetic marble) chess sets are produced in vast quantities and in many shapes and sizes but, like their plastic counterparts, apart from their decorative value they have little merit. Highly polished, well-finished sets are made in the East from alabaster. Often the alabaster is dyed and sold under a number of names. Owing to its soft crystalline structure alabaster is extremely fragile and cannot be considered a good medium from which to make chesspieces.

One of the most attractive modern ceramic sets made in post-war years is produced from fine quality porcelain in the Vista Alegre factory in Portugal. It is a 'bust' type set representing Crusaders and Saracens. Each bust is mounted upon a cone-shaped plinth which, apart from providing height, imparts a certain balance and stability. The pieces are well painted and finished in gold trim.

The bulk of all post-war 'Staunton' type chessmen have been produced in France, where the manufacture is taken very seriously. They are made in several sizes, weighted and baized, and have a fairly good finish, but are in no way comparable with pre-war English Stauntons.

During the past thirty years several types of metal chess sets have been made. They are not popular for the simple reason that as decorative sets they are vastly inferior to old metal sets. It is also true that few serious players like playing with metal pieces.

MATERIALS USED

From the beginning of the fifteenth century the most common substance used for the manufacture of chesspieces was boxwood, a fine close-grained yellow wood obtained from a shrub common to both Europe and Asia. Only the shrub which attains a height of between eight and twelve feet at maturity provides useful

116 Native side bishop in the form of a juggernaut cart from a Delhi set of the 'John' type.

117 Simply but attractively designed pieces made from standard thirty-calibre cartridge used in Springfield rifles.

wood, as the dwarf variety has little or no commercial value as timber.

From the beginning of the eighteenth century ebony was used extensively for making chess sets. This hard black wood is taken from trees which grow in Mauritius, Ceylon, America and India. Only the inner core or 'heartwood' of the tree is sufficiently hard and black to be of use; moving outwards from the core, the wood becomes softer and changes progressively from jet black to yellow. Like boxwood, ebony can be turned or carved to almost any shape or design, and the close grain allows a high degree of finish. Boxwood and ebony used together for opposing sides of the same set provide near perfection in contrast, striking but mellow.

Softwoods used for the manufacture of chesspieces after the beginning of the eighteenth century include apple, pear, cherry and carefully selected types of fir. A skilled turner can use almost any type of wood, but the carver is much more demanding, as only the close-grained woods prove suitable for carving. If other types are used the actual carving has to be very coarse, as otherwise small projecting detail work such as ears, noses and fingers become highly vulnerable and are likely to flake off. In the East, considerable use was made of sandalwood, which is a very close-grained aromatic softwood from a tree common in India.

Sandalwood is light brown in colour, and can be turned or carved to complex shapes and detail; although very soft and easy to use it is extremely durable. It is not normally polished since the application of any polishing agent destroys the aromatic quality of the wood. Bamboo, which is a genus of grass, grows to a height of fifty feet or more; it has been used for many different purposes in the East, including the manufacture of carved chess sets. Owing to the fibrous structure of bamboo it is most difficult (although not impossible) to turn, and it was rarely used in either China or India for the manufacture of chesspieces. Throughout Malaysia bamboo was extensively carved into chess sets which were made for playing purposes, and an altogether outstanding type was produced in Java from carved and painted bamboo.

Ivory, which from remote antiquity has been highly prized, was used in the manufacture of some early European chessmen. They were carved from walrus ivory taken from an animal (*Odobenus osmarus*) which once moved about in vast herds, but was ruthlessly slaughtered for its tusks in medieval times. The walrus has two large tusks projecting downwards from the upper jaw, composed of coarse ivory, with a large cavity running through their centre. The cavity is filled with a hard spongy mass of darker colour; the exterior section of a tusk is creamy white in colour, and has a much finer grain than the core, which in appearance and properties resembles bone.

118 Spanish pieces made from copper and brass early in the twentieth century and with matching board.

119 Pieces of a Chinese seventeenth-century set *(choke-choo-hong-ki)*.

The majority of all Scandinavian eleventh- and twelfth-century ivory treasures are carved from walrus ivory. Fossil remains of walrus tusks found in deposits of Tertiary age are generally referred to as morse ivory.

From about the beginning of the sixteenth century African ivory was used in Europe and by the beginning of the eighteenth was in general use by turners and carvers. African ivory, taken from the African elephant (*Elephas africanus*), has a warm creamy colour which tends to mellow with age, and if exposed to sunlight will turn slightly yellow. Elephant tusks are upper incisor teeth whose roots grow back into the maxillae. As the teeth grow, they become, from a semi-solid pulp, a hard dense substance built up layer by layer, and formed by calcification of the layers. Ivory is composed of vast numbers of microscopic tubes, which are tightly packed and radiate outwards to give the appearance in transverse section of lines of differing colour or striae forming arcs of a circle. Bull ivory can always be distinguished from cow

120 Pieces from an eighteenth-century Meissen porcelain set.

as the grain in bull ivory runs in continuous lines, while in the case of cow ivory the grain is a mass of short broken lines. Although very much smaller than those of the bull, cow tusks are of a slightly superior quality.

African elephants yield the best and largest tusks, which are bigger and superior in quality to tusks taken from Indian beasts, but in some cases, ivory obtained from elephants found in Siam and the Malay States equals in every respect the very best African. There is one important difference between African and Eastern ivory – African mellows with age and tends to become yellow, Eastern bleaches with age, and if exposed to strong sunlight changes in colour from rich cream to chalk white. Almost all European ivory chesspieces are of African ivory, while the vast majority of Eastern sets are of Indian. There are exceptions, and sometimes an Eastern set is found to be carved from African ivory; more often than not, what is thought to be African is in fact Malayan ivory.

Vast quantities of bone were used during the nineteenth century. Although cheap it was difficult to turn or carve, but at that time highly skilled labour was cheaper than fine material. Almost all bone used by manufacturers of chessmen came from sheep. After cleaning, the bone was dried in a kiln to destroy fats and fibrous matter. Well-treated bone, carefully polished, resembles Indian ivory, but a close inspection will reveal numerous pit marks which become more obvious as the surface becomes soiled and dirt becomes embedded in the pits.

Nearly all hardstone chess sets are made from quartz in one of its many forms. Quartz, which is usually a colourless mineral, is found in great abundance in many parts of the world. It is found in metamorphic rocks often rich in gold deposits. Among its varieties are colourless rock crystal, smoky quartz, which can be tinged to resemble yellow topaz, amethyst or sapphire, milky quartz and rose quartz. The mineral known as jasper is red, brown or yellow opaque quartz.

Jade (silicate of lime and magnesia) and jadeite (silicate of sodium and aluminium) are usually referred to collectively as jade. Both minerals are found in China, New Zealand and America, and in prehistoric times were much used for the making of weapons and ornaments. Under the circumstances, it is a little surprising to find so few chesspieces made from this delightful hardstone. Jade is found in various shades of green, brown, blue and white – white jade is generally referred to as 'mutton fat'. It is hard and durable, and when polished is not easily scratched.

CHESSPIECES AND THEIR NAMES

It is possible to relate hundreds of anecdotes concerning the names by which chesspieces are known throughout the world, and how these names were derived. However, no useful purpose is served by repeating unrelated facts unless they can be regarded as irrefutable. As far as can be ascertained, the earliest illustration of Indian chesspieces is found in Hyde's *Mandragorias* (*de Ludis Orientalibus*) (vol. II, 1767); in the illustration the pieces are

121 Pieces from the Swiss side of an unusual Flemish nineteenth-century set with galleys as rooks.

122 Zimmerman cast-iron pieces made in Germany in about 1850 and depicting Gustavus Adolphus versus Ferdinand of Australia.

named: *shah, pherz, pil, asp, ruch,* and *piyade*. Persians have always called the most important chesspiece *shah* (king), while the piece called 'queen' by the western world is named *farzin* (counsellor or monitor), the bishop *pil*, the knight *asp*, the rook *rukh* and the pawn *piyada*. If we consider the earliest names, the only piece which could perhaps lead to confusion is the ship, which later became a chariot. In Sanskrit the piece is called *roka* (for the chariot *ratha*); this became the Persian *rukh*, a name which could also be applied to a warrior or a fierce species of camel — camels were often portrayed in late eighteenth-century Indian and nineteenth-century Burmese chess sets [figure 85]. Countries of the western world translated the earliest names as closely as possible, but in several cases no true or exact translation was possible.

From the sixteenth century much has been written about this; some of it contradictory. For instance it was stated with some authority in the eighteenth century that the very first time a chess bishop was mentioned in English was in 1640, but in 1624 Middleton referred to bishops in his play *The Game of Chesse* (first performed on Friday, 6 August 1624). One should also consider the very fine Lewis chessmen which could never have been anything but bishops, and these were made at least three centuries earlier. The table on page 96 gives the names by which chesspieces are known in the countries where chess is extensively played.

Chaturanga, the name by which chess in its earliest form was known, is pure Sanskrit word compounded from the two Sanskrit words *chatur* (four) and *anga* (a member or component part). As applied to the game of chess, it meant at the outset a miniature Hindu army composed of four distinct species of forces which were originally elephants, horses, ships — later to become chariots — and foot-soldiers. The ships, which often give rise to confusion, were a very necessary part of this mimic army, since melting mountain snow in spring and torrential rains in summer completely flooded the vast plains of the Ganges and those of the Punjab for a considerable part of each year.

Early Persian and Arab scribes never quite agreed on an exact or even approximate date for the change of name from *chaturanga* to *shatranj*, the name by which chess in its medieval form was known. Without doubt ancient Persians changed the Sanskrit word *chaturanga* into *chatrang*, but the Arabs who conquered Persia were without the initial 'c' and concluding 'g' in their alphabet, and were compelled to change or corrupt *chatrang* into *shatranj*, which in course of time found its way into Persian and Indian dialects. Even the poet Firdausi, writing in the tenth century, avoided all mention of a specific date in his account of *shatranj*, so it is reasonable to conclude that it will remain in obscurity.

123 Pieces from a nineteenth-century Indo-Chinese chess set.

THE NAMES OF CHESSPIECES IN VARIOUS LANGUAGES

English	King	Queen	Bishop	Knight	Rook	Pawn
Abyssinian	*Negus*	*Firz*	*Fil*	*Faras*	*Derr*	*Medak*
Arabic	*Shah*	*Firzan*	*Fil*	*Faras*	*Rukhkh*	*Baidaq*
Danish	*Konge*	*Dronning*	*Lober*	*Springer*	*Taarn*	*Bonde*
Dutch	*Koning*	*Koningen*	*Raadsheer*	*Ridder*	*Kasteel*	*Pion*
Finnish	*Kuningas*	*Rouva*	*Juoksija*	*Juoksija*	*Torni*	*Sotamies*
French	*Roi*	*Reine*	*Fou*	*Cavalier*	*Tour*	*Pion*
German	*König*	*Königin*	*Läufer*	*Springer*	*Turm*	*Bauer*
Greek	*Βασιλεύζ*	*Βασίλισσα*	*Τρελλόζ*	*Ίππος*	*Πύργος*	*Πιόνι*
Hungarian	*Király*	*Királyné*	*Futó*	*Ló*	*Bástya*	*Tét*
Indian	*Shah*	*Wazir*	*Fil*	*Asp*	*Rukh*	*Piyada*
Italian	*Re*	*Regina*	*Alfiere*	*Cavaliere*	*Torre*	*Pedina*
Javanese	*Ratu*	*Pateh*	*Mantri*	*Jãran*	*Prahu*	*Bidak*
Moorish	*Shah*	*Leila*	*Fil*	*Faras*	*Rukhkh*	*Hari*
Norwegian	*Konge*	*Dronning*	*Bisp*	*Springer*	*Taarn*	*Bonde*
Persian	*Shah*	*Farzin*	*Pil*	*Asp*	*Rukh*	*Piyada*
Portuguese	*Rei*	*Rainha*	*Delphim*	*Cavallo*	*Roque*	*Pião*
Russian	*Korol*	*Ferz*	*Slon*	*Kon*	*Ladia*	*Peshka*
Spanish	*Rey*	*Reina*	*Alfil*	*Caballo*	*Torre*	*Peon*
Swedish	*Kung*	*Drottningen*	*Löpare*	*Hast*	*Torn*	*Bonde*
Turkish	*Shah*	*Firzan*	*Fil*	*Faras*	*Rukh*	*Baizaq*

MUSEUMS AND BUILDINGS HOUSING INTERESTING CHESSPIECES

As previously stated, chesspieces which are altogether beyond the collector's reach are not discussed in this work, but the following list has been compiled with a view to assisting enthusiasts to see some of these treasures. Recently many celebrated German museums have been resited and reclassified, and where necessary their current locations are given.

BELGIUM
Brussels: Stoclet Collection; Musées Royaux d'Art et d'Histoire

DENMARK
Copenhagen: National Museet; Kunstindustri Museum; Rosenborg Castle
Hellerup: Ole Olesen Collection

FRANCE
Paris: Bibliothèque Nationale; Musée de Cluny; Musée du Louvre

GERMANY
Berlin: Pergamonmuseum (East) includes the Islamic Museum and Bode-Museum which was formerly the Kaiser-Friedrich Museum;
Staatliche Museen Berlin (West), 1 Berlin 33, Arnimallee 23
Cologne: Kunstgewerbe-Museum der Stadt Köln, Hansaring 32a
Dresden: Historisches Museum (Staatliches Historisches Museum); the east wing of the Semper Gallery, Zwinger;
Porzellansammlung, Zwinger, 801, Dresden 1.;
Staatliches Museum für Volkskunst (Landes-museum für sächsische Volkskunst), 806, Dresden 6, Kopckestrasse 1
Frankfurt am Main: Frankfurter Städtische Museen – Museum für Kunsthandwerk, 6 Frankfurt am Main, Schaumainkai 63
Leipzig: Museum des Kunsthandwerks (Grassi Museum), 701, Leipzig 1
Nuremberg: Germanisches Nationalmuseum, Kornmarkt 1
Osnabrück: Bischöfliches Diözesanmuseum, im Domkreuzgang
Quedlinburg: Schlossmuseum – Städtisches Museum, 43 Quedlinburg, Schlossberg 1
Regensburg (Ratisbon): St Ulrichs Kirche
Schwerin: Staatliches Museum, 27 Schwerin, Am Alten Garten
Sigmaringen: Fürstlich Hohenzollernsches Museum, Schloss

HOLLAND
The Hague: Huis Ten Bosch

ITALY
Fabriano: Possente Collection
Florence: Museo Nazionale
Naples: Museo Nazionale
Ravenna: Public Museum
Rome: The Vatican

NORWAY
Oslo: Etnografike Museet

SWEDEN
Lund: Kulturhistoriska Museet
Stockholm: National Museum; Slott Skokloster; Statens Historiska Museum

GREAT BRITAIN
Dublin: Petrie Collection; R. Bale Collection
Edinburgh: Museum of the Society of Antiquaries of Scotland; National Museum of Antiquities of Scotland
London: The British Museum; The London Museum; Victoria and Albert Museum
Nottingham: Art Gallery and Museum
Oxford: The Pitt-Rivers Museum
Salisbury: Salisbury Museum
Stoke-on-Trent: Etruria Museum
York: Yorkshire Museum

TURKEY
Istanbul: The Treasury Museum

UNITED STATES OF AMERICA
Baltimore: Maryland Historical Society; Walters Gallery
Brooklyn: Brooklyn Museum
Cleveland: Cleveland Public Library
Minneapolis: Minneapolis Institute of Fine Art
New York: Manhattan Chess Club; Marshall's Chess Club; Metropolitan Museum
Philadelphia: University Museum
San Francisco: N. H. De Young Memorial Museum
Washington DC: Georgetown University Museum; United States National Museum
State of Washington: Maryhill Museum (on the Columbia River about 120 miles from Portland, Oregon)

MEXICO DF
Museo Nacionale

Good illustrations of early playing pieces may be seen in the following works:
Caxton *The Game and Play of Chess* (English translation of Cessolis), 1480
Chessmen from Publicius, *Ars Oratoria,* 1482
Chessmen from Lucena, 1497
Chessmen from *Damiano's Problems,* 1512 (and fifth edition 1524–50)
Chessmen from Kobel, after Massmann, 1520
Chessmen from Egenolff, 1536
Chessmen from *Grecco's Problems,* 1576
Chessmen from Selenus, 1616
French chesspieces are illustrated in the *Encyclopédie Méthodique,* 1792